Twayne's United States Authors Series

EDITOR OF THIS VOLUME

Sylvia E. Bowman

Indiana University

American Indian Poetry

TUSAS 334

AMERICAN INDIAN POETRY

By HELEN ADDISON HOWARD

TWAYNE PUBLISHERS
A DIVISION OF G. K. HALL & CO., BOSTON

Copyright © 1979 by G. K. Hall & Co.

Published in 1979 by Twayne Publishers,
A Division of G. K. Hall & Co.
All Rights Reserved

Printed on permanent/durable acid-free paper and bound
in the United States of America

First Printing

Library of Congress Cataloging in Publication Data

Howard, Helen Addison.
American Indian poetry.

(Twayne's United States authors series; TUSAS 334)

Bibliography: pp. 175–87
Includes index.
1. American poetry—20th century—
History and criticism. 2. Indians in literature.
3. Indian poetry—History and criticism. I. Title
PS324.H68   811'.5'09897   78-32103
ISBN 0-8057-7271-5

To Matt
Whose help and
friendly criticism
have been invaluable

Contents

About the Author

Helen Addison Howard selected for her master's thesis, "Recent Versified Transcriptions and Imitations of the Poetry of the American Indians," for her Master of Arts degree in 1933 at the University of Southern California. *War Chief Joseph,* her first book, was published in 1941, assisted in the research by Dan L. McGrath, and reissued as a Bison Book (1964). It was dramatized for American Indian Day over KFI-NBC radio in 1949 with ex-Governor Ronald Reagan as narrator. Other books include *Northwest Trail Blazers* (1963); *Saga of Chief Joseph* (1965/75), (a new revised edition of *War Chief Joseph*), was reissued as a Bison Book (1978); *American Frontier Tales,* (1979).

In addition, Miss Howard has published many scholarly and popular historical magazine articles; equestrian and general magazine features; several short stories; and has contributed three ethnohistory articles on Northwestern Plateau tribes to the five-volume general reference *Dictionary of Indian Tribes of the Americas* (1979). She was editor of Chapter 14 in *Frontier Omnibus* (1962). Since 1969 she has been a book reviewer for *Journal of the West* and is now a member of this quarterly's Editorial Advisory Board under the aegis of Kansas State University. Six articles have appeared in the Journal's special topical issues from 1971 to 1979 inclusive. Miss Howard resides with her husband, Ben Overland, a retired business man, in Burbank, California.

Preface

This study was undertaken to introduce the modern reader to a rich heritage of neglected literature: Native American verse. Although much has been written in the past about Indian poetry, it is almost unknown by today's generation of readers. As Louis Untermeyer has observed: "Indian poetry is the earliest art of which any trace can be found in America and it is the last to have received the attention of students."[1] He cited three reasons for this condition: prejudice on the part of the government in not allowing Indian songs to be sung in reservation schools, the difficulties of translation, and the radical differences in tribal traditions which confused researchers even more than the language barrier did.

The first serious study of Indian poetry was Henry Rowe Schoolcraft's Indian history, published in 1851, which included a few samples of Chippewa songs. The next serious attempt was that of J. S. Brisbin, whose article "Poetry of Indians" appeared in Harper's Magazine in June, 1878. Brisbin explained the difficulties of translating Indian verse, and he presented some translations as examples. In 1883, Daniel G. Brinton began his studies about Native American authors, and by 1890, his research had culminated in the *Library of Aboriginal American Literature*. This eight-volume set included Horatio Hale's "Iroquois Book of Rites" and Brinton's translations from Lenape (Delaware) Indian literature that contained poetic passages.

Another outstanding researcher, Alice C. Fletcher, started collecting, translating, and publishing Omaha tribal songs as early as 1884 with the aid of a head chief's son, Francis La Flesche. Her article, "Indian Songs—Personal Studies of Indian Life," published in the *Century Magazine* of January, 1894, analyzed some characteristics of Indian poems. A pioneer interpreter, Mary H. Austin, became convinced by 1900 that there was a relationship existing "between aboriginal and later American forms"[2] of poetry, and she began writing "re-expressions" of Indian songs about 1905. These poetic efforts were rejected by the magazines of the period because there was "no excuse for this sort of thing."[3] In 1907, Natalie Curtis's notable work, *The Indians' Book,* a source volume of translations, was offered to an indifferent world.

In addition to the foregoing studies, the work of several ethnologists deserves mention. Foremost among their literary achievements is Washington Matthews's translation of "The Mountain Chant: A Navajo Ceremony" in the *Annual Report* of the Bureau of American Ethnology for 1887; and other monographs of his are referred to in this text. The next year, Franz Boas published a paper about Chinook songs in the *Journal of American Folk-Lore* and one about the Central Eskimo in the Ethnology Bureau's *6th Annual Report.* In 1891, James Mooney's remarkable "Sacred Formulas of the Cherokees" appeared in translation in the bureau's *7th Annual Report.* Frank Russell did a study of the Pima Indians for the Bureau of American Ethnology in 1908. More recent is the *Songs of the Tewa,* translated and printed in 1933 by the eminent ethnologist, Herbert J. Spinden. Another anthropologist who possessed a rare literary gift and whose knowledge of the Papago language enabled her to translate their myths, legends, songs, and chants is Dr. Ruth Murray Underhill. Her finest volume (for literary style) is *Singing for Power: The Song Magic of the Papago Indians of Southern Arizona* (1938; reissued, 1968).

The American literati mostly remained indifferent to native poetry until 1911. After Austin delivered an address on the subject before the Poetry Society that year, Indian verse began to receive some notice. According to her statement, it was then considered a new form and began to be called *vers libre.* Interest in Indian poetry was also aroused following the publication in 1918 of George Cronyn's anthology *The Path on the Rainbow* which was, as Louis Untermeyer noted, the "first comprehensive general collection of aboriginal verse in translation."[4] Native poetry, however, did not become a topic of controversy until Untermeyer's review "The Indian as Poet," in the *Dial* (March, 1919) attacked Cronyn's anthology, leading to a warm defense of Cronyn by Austin.

Preface

Since then, Indian verse has been coming into its own through the efforts of eight modern poets of literary reputation—Alice C. Fletcher, Frances Densmore, Mary H. Austin, Natalie Curtis (Burlin), Alice C. Henderson, Constance L. Skinner, Lew Sarett, and Eda Lou Walton—whose work is critically analyzed in this study. The most significant recent anthology is Dr. A Grove Day's *The Sky Clears* (1951; reprinted, 1964). This comprehensive volume embraces poetic translations from the Arctic Eskimos to the Aztecs and the Mayas of old Mexico.

Nonetheless, there has been a conspicuous lack of critical treatment of Native American poetry. With the exception of Professor Nellie Barnes's scholarly study *American Indian Verse, Characteristics of Style*, which was done at the University of Kansas in 1921, and an analysis of the Indian poetic impulse found in Austin's work *The American Rhythm* (1923; revised in 1930), there has been almost nothing of import except for some critical evaluation of poetic types in Dr. Spinden's "Essay on American Indian Poetry" (1933), and a few analytical comments in Professor Day's *The Sky Clears* and in Dr. Harry Paige's study of Teton Sioux songs (1970).

Although Austin found a relationship between Indian poetry and modern verse in the "extraordinary likeness between much of this native product and the recent (1918) work of the Imagists, *vers librists*, and other literary fashionables,"[5] the purpose of this monograph is not to trace the influence of Indian poetry on American free verse but to summarize the dominant traits of Indian verse and to show the influence of native poetic forms on the work of the modern poets previously named. Nor is this study intended to compare aboriginal American and European forms of prosody.

Since only a few non-Indians, ethnologists, folklorists, linguists, and a small coterie of white American poets are knowledgeable about indigenous poetry, various aspects of this curiously unknown lore should be explored to bridge the literary gap. As Professor Day has so aptly stated in his volume *The Sky Clears*: "The poems of the North American Indians—songs and chants composed by the Indians themselves, which have been translated into English by experts—can seldom be fully appreciated unless the reader has some understanding of the origins of this native verse and the human needs and desires that brought it into being."[6]

For the non-Indian to comprehend such poetry, the words of a song-poem should be interwoven with music, the beat of a drum, the rattle of a gourd, and the stamp or shuffle of the dancers' moccasined feet. Moreover, the listener should have a knowledge of the myths and legends and of the customs and life-style that form a background for the words and the music. To enrich this background knowledge, succinct descriptions are included of the ethnohistory of those tribes whose poetry is under study. The reader must also have an understanding of the metrical style that affects Indian poetry.

There are several kinds of poets who deal with native verse. One of these used the Indian as a subject or theme for poetic inspiration, as John Neihardt did in the *Song of the Indian Wars* (1925), or as Hartley Burr Alexander collected in his polished, academic volume, *God's Drum and Other Cycles* (1927), or like Amy Lowell's experimentations in "Songs of the Pueblos" in *Ballads for Sale* (1927). These types of metrical composers are not considered in this monograph, for only those works of our best poets are reviewed whose most serious work is of two kinds: free translations from the Indian originals (or perhaps better, "transcriptions" in the sense in which that word is used in music), such as Natalie Curtis's *The Indians' Book* (1907); and interpretations using subjects and rhythms drawn from aboriginal life and song, such as that section of Lew Sarett's volume *Many Many Moons* (1920) in which he "endeavored to maintain steadily and accurately the consciousness of the genuine American Indian of today."[7]

This brief survey of the poetic art of the North American Indians is intended as an introduction to both the earlier works and to the nineteenth-century preserved metrical compositions of Indian bards from representative tribes in all cultural areas throughout the United States. If some tribes are emphasized more than others, it is either because their songs and chants have more literary merit, or because more of their poetry has been collected and translated. For instance, in the Bitter Root Valley of western Montana, no attempt was made to record the poems of the Flathead or kindred tribes of the Salishan Nation; and unfortunately, the creations of Indian bards in other regions have suffered a like fate. One scholarly study by Alan P. Merriam, *Ethnomusicology of the Flathead Indians* (1967), does present the music but the songs were chanted without words. The meaning of a few poems with words was unknown to Dr. Merriam's Indian informants.

In summary, my threefold purpose is (1) to introduce the reader to American Indian verse by a discussion of its style and by citing for comparison poetic samples from the work of the best translators, interpreters, or imitators; (2) to show how well the subject matter, free verse form, and rhythm peculiar to native American prosody has been preserved in the work of three major translators and five major interpreters; (3) to evaluate the cultural contribution made to our American heritage by translations and interpretations of the Indians' verse through a critical and analytical examination of their relative merits. Furthermore, this study may help to advance cultural knowledge of the Native American race which has made numerous other contributions to Western civilization.

Helen Addison Howard

Burbank, California

Acknowledgments

The author wishes to express sincere appreciation for the invaluable aid and cooperation of the following individuals and institutions without whose assistance and resources this study would have been impossible: Mrs. Lu Artz, Reference Librarian, Burbank Public Library, Burbank, California; Miss H. W. Azhderian, Head Reference Librarian, Doheny Memorial Library, University of Southern California, Los Angeles, for granting permission to the author to use freely her Master of Arts thesis on American Indian Poetry; *TUSAS* editor, Dr. Sylvia E. Bowman; Mrs. Ruth M. Christensen, Librarian, Southwest Museum, Los Angeles, California; Miss Janet Hawkins, Assistant to Registrar, Huntington Library, San Marino, California; Los Angeles Public Library; New Research Library, University of California at Los Angeles; Dr. T. M. Pearce, Professor-Emeritus of English, University of New Mexico, Albuquerque; Mrs. Charlotte Tufts, former Librarian, Southwest Museum, Los Angeles, California, and to the Glendale and Pasadena Public Libraries.

Grateful acknowledgment is also made to the following publishers, authors, or other owners of copyright for permission to reprint quotations from their material:

Austin, Mary H. *The American Rhythm*. Boston and New York: Houghton Mifflin Company, 1930. Reprinted by permission of the publishers.

Curtis, Natalie. *The Indians' Book*. New York: Dover Publications, Inc., 1968. Reprinted by permission of the publishers.

Day, A. Grove. *The Sky Clears*. Lincoln: University of Nebraska Press, Bison Book edition, 1964. Reprinted by permission of Dr. Day.

Henderson, Alice Corbin. *Red Earth*. Chicago: Ralph Fletcher Seymour, 1920. Reprinted by permission of Mrs. Edgar L. Rossin.

Sarett, Lew. *Box of God*. Copyright, 1922, by Henry Holt and

Chronology

ALICE CUNNINGHAM FLETCHER

1838 Alice Cunningham Fletcher born March 15 in Cuba during temporary sojourn there of parents Thomas G. and Lucia Adeline (Jenks) Fletcher.

1904 Monograph on *The Hako: A Pawnee Ceremony,* assisted by James R. Murie, and by Edwin S. Tracy, published in *Twenty-second Annual Report,* Bureau of American Ethnology, Part 2 (Washington).

1911 Monograph *The Omaha Tribe* published; assisted by adopted son, Francis La Flesche. *Twenty-Seventh Annual Report,* Bureau of American Ethnology (Washington).

1923 Died April 6 at her home in Washington, D.C.

FRANCES DENSMORE

1867 Frances Densmore born May 21 in Red Wing, Minnesota; daughter of Benjamin and Sarah Adelaide (Greenland) Densmore.

1910 Publication of "Chippewa Music," *Bulletin* 45 (Washington, D.C.).

1913 Publication of "Chippewa Music II," *Bulletin* 53 (Washington, D.C.).

1929 "Papago Music," *Bulletin* 90 (Washington, D.C.).

1957 Died June 5 in Red Wing.

MARY HUNTER AUSTIN

1868 Mary Hunter born September 9, in Carlinville, Illinois; second daughter of Captain George Hunter and Susannah Savilla (Graham) Hunter.

1923 *The American Rhythm* (New York); revised edition, 1930 (Boston, New York).

1934 Died August 13 in Santa Fe.

NATALIE CURTIS (BURLIN)

1875   Natalie Curtis born April 26 in New York City; daughter of Edward and Augusta Lawler (Stacey) Curtis.

1907   *The Indians' Book* (New York); second edition, 1923 (New York); reissued, 1935, 1950, 1968 (New York).

1921   Died October 23 in Paris, France.

ALICE CORBIN (HENDERSON)

1881   Alice Corbin born April 16 in St. Louis, Missouri, daughter of Fillmore Mallory and Lulu Hebe (Carradine) Corbin.

1920   Volume of Indian and New Mexico verse, *Red Earth,* published (Chicago); reissued, 1921 (Chicago).

1949   Died July 18 in Santa Fé, New Mexico.

CONSTANCE LINDSAY SKINNER

1879   Constance Lindsay Skinner born in northern British Columbia, daughter of factor Robert James Skinner at Hudson's Bay Trading Post on Peace River, and of his wife Anne (Lindsay) Skinner.

1930   *Songs of the Coast Dwellers,* Indian verse (New York).

1937   Editor, Rivers of America Series for Farrar and Rinehart in New York; position continued until her death.

1939   Died March 27 in New York City.

LEW SARETT

1888   Lew Sarett born May 16 in Chicago, son of Rudolph and Jeanette (Block) Sarett.

1920   Publication of first volume of verse, *Many Many Moons* (New York).

1922   *The Box of God* published, second volume of Indian verse (New York).

1925   *Slow Smoke,* Indian poems (New York).

1954   Died August 17 in Gainesville, Florida.

EDA LOU WALTON

1894   Eda Lou Walton born January 19 in Deming, New Mexico;

daughter of William Bell and Leoline (Ashenfelter) Walton.

1925 "American Indian Poetry," *The American Anthropologist,* XXVII (January), coauthored with T. T. Waterman; later contributed other articles to same journal.

1926 *Dawn Boy* (New York), volume of Blackfoot and Navajo songs; introduction by Witter Bynner.

1961 Died December 9 at Oakland, California.

CHAPTER 1

The Style of Indian Poetry

IN order to appreciate Indian verse, the reader must first understand certain features peculiar to its style. Nearly all Indian poetry is communal. Because it is intended to be chanted or sung with interpretive and dramatic gestures, specific words and phrases are few and fragmentary. As a result, the poems often sound crude and inadequate to ears accustomed to the poetry of Western Civilization. The ideas expressed may represent only the high points of an emotional flight, or they may symbolize a great situation. The Indian, like the Chinese, thinks and expresses himself in symbols. A single Indian word may represent an idea whose expression in English would require a whole sentence. These ideas must either be interpreted against a background of myth or legend, or be supplemented by music, chants, and dance postures and gestures.

I *Poetry is Power*

Indian poetry is purely vocal, and the poem's meaning and mood are expressed as much by its melodic quality as by its verbal content. The American Indian is very musical and has songs for all situations. These include religious songs, hunting songs, medicine songs, dream songs, lullabies, love songs, war songs, and social dance songs. Other songs are for gambling games, personal achievements, and gifts. There are songs of thanks, songs for spirits or deities, songs of mourning, and songs to heal the sick. Most of the ritual poems are religious or magical in nature, and they are therefore the treasured and often secret literary possessions of an individual or of a tribal society. Essentially, Indian poetry is poetry with a purpose, for poetic expression meant magical power to the Indian.

21

Fletcher has observed that all types of songs were an attempt by man to communicate with the supernatural:

The invisible voice could reach the invisible power that permeates all nature, animating all natural forms. As success depended upon help from this mysterious power, in every avocation, in every undertaking, and in every ceremonial, the Indian appealed to this power through song. When a man went forth to hunt, that he might secure food and clothing for his family, he sang songs to insure the assistance of the unseen power in capturing the game. In like manner, when he confronted danger and death, he sang that strength might be given him to meet his fate unflinchingly. In gathering the healing herbs and in administering them, song brought the required efficacy. When he planted, he sang, in order that the seed might fructify and the harvest follow. In his sports, in his games, when he wooed and when he mourned, song alike gave zest to pleasure and brought solace to his suffering. In fact, the Indian sang in every experience of life from his cradle to his grave.[1]

For example, a chant common to all tribes whose existence depended on hunting is the Nez Perce song "Twi-tash" (The Bear Hunter).[2] To propitiate the spirits, the singer denies responsibility for the bear's death; then he seeks absolution through an ingenious alibi!

> This bear was my friend
> Living in the great woods,
> I did not kill him,
> Too—na—a—na—ta—hoe.
> He committed self-death
> By coming before the arrow.
> Gus—nee—whey, oh—ta—hee—na—ho—gus—hee—
> Perhaps hunger that was in my camp
> He knew, and came that our lives
> Might be strengthened.
> I did not kill this bear,
> My friend of the woods,
> I did not kill this bear,
> My friend of the woods.

An interesting comparison to this song is the "Medicine-Song of the Grizzly-Bear,"[3] which has been translated literally by Edward S. Curtis:

> Híya! Dawn! Híya! Dawn is moving and passes me, going!
> Híya! Dawn! Híya! Dawn is moving and passes me, going!
> Híya! Dawn! Híya! Dawn is moving

Curtis explains that in the Indian's mind, these words create a picture of a mortally wounded grizzly bear who is sitting facing the East with his back against a tree. He sings while wondering if he will live to see the sun rise, but he fears to see it because a "wound is at its worst just at sunrise, and at noon, and at sunset," as the injury feels hotter at those times. Then he sees the sun's beautiful rays shining over the mountains and striking the treetop where he is sitting. The rays take on the colors of the rainbow as well as the color of his dark, dried blood. The sun passes over him for many days, and each time he becomes weaker as the sun takes part of his life.[4]

"The music of the songs is delightfully rhythmic and entrancing," Curtis comments, "and seems peculiarly appropriate to a religion so largely emotional and hypnotic." His volume, which is based on field studies, gives the music and the words of a number of Nez Perce songs which he describes as striking in Indian imagery. He presents them "with a translation of the words and a description, literally recorded, of the picture which each produces on the imaginative mind of the Indian."[5]

The world of nature is such an intrinsic part of his everyday life that the Indian personifies every aspect of the outdoors in his poetic expression. The birds that fly and the beasts that walk or crawl, the sun and the moon, the thunder and the lightning, the waters of the earth, and the star people of the heavens—all of these compose the essence of native poetic thought.[6] Lew Sarett points out that "the North American Indian . . . has no special form of expression called poetry. . . . Poetic beauty, sometimes simple and stark but very real, enfolds all his modes of expression, his songs and his dances, his religious practices, his feasts and chants, his superstitions and folklore and legends. In a sense his poetry is implied, rather than expressed."[7]

II *The "Inside Song"*

What the Indians call an "inside song" is another peculiarity of their verse, because the full meaning of a poem is never expressed in the words alone. To an Indian, the words are only a shorthand note to this "inside song." "It [the inside song] may be a long story, actual or mythical," according to Mary Austin, "a dramatic episode or the progressive emotional phases going on in the mind of the poet—any one of these giving rise to the music, dance, and phrase that inseparably constitute an Indian song."[8] Thus, a large part of a man's life experience may be expressed in a single sentence; yet, if the poem is to be comprehensible to the non-Indian reader, the story or episode behind the poem must be known.

An example of a mythical story or inside song that has given rise to a poem may be cited from the Navajo "Song of the Horse." The inside song connected with the poem concerns the Sun-God, who has five horses: one of turquoise; one of white shell; one of pearl shell; one of red shell; and one of coal. As the Sun-God rides across the skies each day from the East to the West, he carries the shining, golden disk of the sun. In fair weather, the Sun-God, Johano-ai, rides either his turquoise steed, his white shell charger, or his pearl charger; but on dark stormy days he rides his pony of red shell or of coal. All kinds of precious hides are spread beneath the hooves of the horses. This imagery probably expresses both the colors of the sky and of the clouds.

The Sun-God feeds his coursers on flower blossoms, and he gives them of the "mingled waters" to drink. These waters, used in Navajo rites, are holy. They come from the four corners of the world—from springs, snow, and hail. Instead of dust, the Sun-God's chargers raise the "glittering grains of mineral" such as the Navajos use in religious ceremonies. ("Glittering grains" supposedly refer to bits of turquoise and other precious stones). When the horses shake or roll, these symbolical "glittering grains" fly from them; when the horses run, the sacred pollen offered to the Sun-God surrounds them like a mist.

The Navajos believe that the mist on the horizon is the pollen offered to the gods. Therefore, standing amidst his herds, a Navajo will sing of the Sun-God's horses so that he too can have steeds like those of Johano-ai. He will scatter the holy pollen in order to call down the blessing and protection of the Sun-God on his ponies.[9]

Song of the Horse[10]

How joyous his neigh!

Lo, the Turquoise Horse of Johano-ai,

How joyous his neigh,

There on precious hides outspread standeth he;
How joyous his neigh,
There on tips of fair fresh flowers feedeth he;
How joyous his neigh,
There of mingled waters holy drinketh he;
How joyous his neigh.
There he spurneth dust of glittering grains;
How joyous his neigh,
There in mist of sacred pollen hidden, all hidden he;
How joyous his neigh,
There his offspring many grow and thrive for evermore;
How joyous his neigh!

III   *Other Features of Native American Verse*

Besides the inside song, there are other unique aspects of Indian verse, which are largely matters of form or construction. Indian poems are generally brief, and they begin without introduction or exposition. A typical illustration is a song composed by the famous Sitting Bull, who was both a medicine man and a warrior of the Uncpapa Sioux or Dakota Nation, and one of the Indian leaders in the Custer fight. When he was a boy, his life was saved by a dream in which a bird forewarned him of an encounter with a grizzly bear. When he awoke, he heard the lumbering animal's approach; but he managed to save himself by feigning death beneath the bear's investigating paws. Later, he composed this chant to his friend the yellowhammer:

Pretty bird, you saw me and took pity on me;
You wished me to survive among the people.
O Bird People, from this day always you shall be my
     relatives.[11]

Native American poetry occasionally shows a tendency to rhyme because vocables that are similar in sound are frequently found at the end of each phrase.[12] When the words do not fit the rhythm of the music, the Indian bard often uses syllables composed of vowels instead of words. These vowels, both open and nasal, are modified by an initial consonant such as *h* or *y*, as in *hae* (pronounced *hay*), *ha, he, ho, hi, hu*.[13] The h is used for gentleness; the y expresses derision or warlike feeling. The Indian poet also introduces syllables between parts of a word whose vocables would otherwise break or injure the cadence of the song.[14]

The use of vocables to complete the ryhthm is clearly demonstrated in "The Rock Wren and the Rattlesnake"[15] as translated from the Nez Perce by L. V. McWhorter:

You have a blunt nose,
Your head is flat and ugly,
You crawl in among the rocks,
Your home is in the dark ground,
Your color is dull and faded,
Wan-a-hey—wan-a-yay.

You are bad all the time,
Nobody like you,
Your breath is poisonous,
Your bite is deadly,
You hide like a coward.

Come out from your hiding,
I am not afraid of you!
Wan-a-hey, wan-a-hey,
Wan-a-yay, wan-a-yay,
Wan-a-yay!

IV General Characteristics of Indian Music

Although all Indian music was rhythmical, it usually lacked harmony. In rare cases, however, such as those found among the Cherokee and other southern tribes, harmonic effects were produced by the resonant voices of 200 or 300 persons who, joining in a choral, carried the melody in octaves by soprano, tenor, and bass vocalizing. By contrast, investigators discovered that plural singing was generally in unison among the Plains and some northwest coast tribes. The women sang in high, falsetto tones usually an octave above the male voices. However, singing two or more melodic lines simultaneously was rare except for drone polyphony in which "one voice sustains a single tone while another sings a melody."[16] Both Frances Densmore and Wilhelmine Driver, specialists in Indian music and dances, "found that although rhythms were often fairly complex, regular measure or bar lengths occurred less frequently than uneven bar lengths and asymmetrical rhythmic patterns."[17] Alice C. Fletcher, collector of Indian music and songs, noted that the rhythm of the drum often differed from the rhythm of the song. For example, the drum might be played in 2/4 time and the song be sung in 3/4 time. "The beat governs the bodily movements," Fletcher explained, while "the song voices the emotion of the appeal."[18]

The primary musical instruments used were whistles, drums, flutes (properly flageolets), rattles of the calabash type, and the hollow wooden rattle of the northwest coast. Drums had skin heads and varied in size and structure. For instance, on the northwest coast a plank or box served as a drum. Whistles were made of bone, wood, or pottery. Some whistles were capable of producing two or more tones, and they were employed in a few ceremonies. Flageolets and whistles were widely distributed, the former being used to accompany songs of certain Pueblo ceremonies. Rattles were universal among the tribes, but the only melodic instruments were flutes and flageolets, which were usually played by young men for courting or love charms.[19]

Frances Densmore noted certain variations in the instruments used among the different tribal groups, such as a northwest coast tribe's hollow wooden rattle and the notched stick rattles in the southwest. She explained:

The notched-stick is rested on a resonator to amplify the sound, this varying in different localities. The Acoma use a squash for this purpose, the Utes use a shallow basket or a sheet of tin, the Yaqui use a half-gourd, and the Papago use an ordinary household basket. A shallow box was used as a resonator in recording songs that required this accompaniment [as some resonators were not feasible for the recording machine]. This instrument is used by the Acoma with only two dances, one being a "sacred" dance and the other a social dance. . . . The history and distribution of the notched-stick rattle is interesting, the earliest example, so far as known, having been used in Confucian ceremonies in China. It is found in various forms in Japan, Mexico, Guatemala, Puerto Rico, and other countries, and was used by the Negroes in Africa and by the Maya Indians.[20]

The hollow wooden rattle was an instrumental variation devised by the Makah tribe of Neah Bay, Washington. Seashore pebbles put in a long box were rocked back and forth across a log as an accompaniment to the Thunderbird Dance. Men fashioned and played the instruments, originally used mostly as percussion accompaniment to the singing. Stringed instruments were unknown in North America before European contact with the natives, although a hunting bow sometimes served to produce rhythm.

Music, like poetry, was valued for its magical power rather than for its aesthetic component. The Indian had no conception of an objective presentation of musical compositions.[21] Wilhelmine Driver noted that, although Indian artistic achievement has shown great diversity of "creative and performing styles. . . . their music, . . . song and dance must serve either a practical or useful end."[22] However, music was also composed for group or individual pleasure to accompany the social dances which were common among the tribes.

Discussing the relationship of words to music, Alice Fletcher has stated that:

Where vocables are added to fill out the measure of a line. or are exclusively used in singing of a phrase or a song, they are regarded as being unchangeable as words, and no liberties are ever taken with them. The same treatment of words in their relation to the musical phrase is observed in the secular songs of tribes. In those sung by the various societies at their gatherings, or those which accompany the vocations of men or women in love songs, war songs, hunting songs, or mystery songs, the musical phrase in every instance fixes the rhythm and measure, and the words and vocables are made to conform to it. In many of these songs the words are few, but they have been carefully chosen with reference to their capability of conveying the thought of the composer in a manner that, to the native's mind, will be poetic, not prosaic.[23]

In an additional explanation of the characteristics of music and songs, Fletcher wrote:

Music of each ceremony has its peculiar rhythm, so have the classes of songs which pertain to individual acts: fasting and prayer, setting of traps, hunting, courtship, playing of games, facing and defying death. . . . In structure Indian song is a short, melodic phrase built on related tones which we denominate chord lines, repeated with more or less variation, grouped into clauses, and correlated into periods. The compass of the songs varies from 1 to 3 octaves.[24]

She summarized the difficulties encountered in the study of Indian music along with its concomitant rewards:

It has always been difficult for a listener of another race to catch an Indian song, as the melody is often "hidden by overpowering noise." When, however, this difficulty has been overcome, these untrammeled expresions of emotions present a rich field in which to observe the growth of musical form and the beginning of musical thinking. They form an important chapter in the development of music. Apart from this historic value, these songs offer to the composer a wealth of melodic and rhythmic movements, and that peculiar inspiration which heretofore has been obtained solely from the folk songs of Europe.[25]

V *Indian and Greek Verse Forms*

While Indian verse makes use of many of the general stylistic devices found in Greek forms, there is one outstanding difference. The similarities of form include a definite repetitive rhythmic pattern, sonority of sound, assonance, and occasional alliteration and rhyme. The chief difference between the Indian and Greek forms lies in the expression of the image. Alice Corbin Henderson explains:

Indian poetry, in its most characteristic form, is at the opposite pole from . . . the usual occidental lyric, which gives a double image, i.e., the original emotional stimulus *through* the thought or emotion aroused by it. Indian poetry is seldom selfconscious to this degree. It gives the naked image, or symbol, which is itself the emotional stimulus. The distinction is subtle, but one who would interpret or translate Indian verse must perceive it.[26]

In other words, in European poetry the writer develops a mood or presents exposition to generate a feeling later in the composition. But the native bard simply names his image, disregarding the establishment of exposition, or the development of a mood or a feeling, as in the Navajo "Song of the Rain Chant."[27]

> Far as man can see,
> Comes the rain,
> Comes the rain with me.

For the non-Indian reader to comprehend the meaning of this poem, it is necessary for him to know that the poem refers to the Rain-Youth, a Navajo deity, who comes down from the Rain-Mountain with the rain and sings as he journeys. In Navajo mythology, a storm with thunder and lightning is the Male-Rain, while a gentle shower symbolizes the Female-Rain. The two hold a rendezvous on the hills and from this union all vegetation grows upon the earth. The Rain-Mountain, home of the Rain-Youth, lies far to the west of Zuñi Pueblo. The rain songs were given to the Navajos by the Rain-Youth who composed them. The full seven stanzas of this chant tell of the rain feathers in the Divine One's hair as he descends from the mountain with the rain and comes through the corn and the pollen which conceal him as birds chirp for joy with the rain. Human beings see only a mist, as the Rain-Youth is hidden by pollen to earthly eyes. It is well for a Divine One to be covered by holy pollen for such pollen the Navajos believe is "an emblem of peace."[28]

VI Indian Lyric Poetry

On the subject of form, Nellie Barnes has found that the chief characteristic movement of the Indian lyric is "recessional." By "recessional" she means that the motif "appears at the opening of the song, with the emotional intensity or emphasis gradually dying away toward the close."[29] This movement occurs in the

Navajo "Song of the Hogans,"[30] and also in the Zuñi "Coyote and the Locust."[31]

> Locust, locust, playing a flute,
>> Locust, locust, playing a flute!
> Away up on the pine-tree bough,
>> Closely clinging,
> Playing a flute,
>> Playing a flute!

In a modification of this "recessional" lyric type, the motif opens the song, is repeated at regularly recurring intervals throughout, and ends abruptly without the refrain. This type of "recessional" is a transitional and a more barbaric kind.

On the other hand, the "forward movement finds its most natural place in the ballads and in those ritualistic poems which anticipate dramatic gesture or action"[32] which we find in the "Daylight Song"[33] from "The Hako." In this song, the emphasis increases by repetition toward the close of the chant when the dawn appears:

> Day is here! Day is here, is here!
> Arise, my son, lift thine eyes.
>> Day is here! Day is here, is here!
> Day is here! Day is here, is here!
> Look up, my son, and see the day.
>> Day is here! Day is here, is here!
> Day is here! Day is here, is here!

In her volume *American Indian Love Lyrics*,[34] Professor Barnes classified four distinctive forms or patterns of construction in Indian lyric poetry. The first of these is iterative, in which the repetitions occur in each stanza either at the opening or close. The Navajo "Mountain Song" is an example of this type:

> Song from the Mountain Chant[35]
>
> Thereof he telleth.
>
> Now of the Holy Youth,
>> Thereof he telleth.

> Moccasins decked with black,
>   Thereof he telleth.
>
> And richly broidered dress,
>   Thereof he telleth.
>
> Arm-bands of eagle feathers,
>   Thereof he telleth.
>
> And now the rain-plumes,
>   Thereof he telleth.

The myth accompanying the ceremony tells of the Holy Youth who loved a mortal maiden. So that he might make her divine and then marry her, he sang holy songs over her. When she became the Holy Woman, the pair gave the chants to the Navajo to use in a ceremony to cure illness. The medicine man would make a colored sand picture on the ground and chant the song-poem.

The second "thought-rhythm" pattern is alternating in design; the repetitions are carried alternately from the first line in the first stanza to the first line in the second stanza, from the second line in the first stanza to the second line in the second stanza, etc. This type is especially well illustrated in the graceful lilt of the Hopi "Katzina" songs:

Korosta Katzina Song[36]

> Yellow butterflies,
> Over the blossoming virgin corn,
>   With pollen-painted faces
> Chase one another in brilliant throng.
>
> Blue butterflies,
> Over the blossoming virgin beans,
>   With pollen-painted faces
> Chase one another in brilliant streams.

This song of four stanzas was composed at the turn of the century by Koianimptiwa, a young Hopi poet, to celebrate the Hopi Corn-Dance in May. He explained to the translator that the butterflies had dusted themselves with pollen for their flight over the blossoming corn and bean fields. The Indians representing "Katzinas"—intermediary deities who brought Hopi prayers to the gods—wore rainbow-painted masks for the dancing ceremony. The poem also demonstrates the Indian's use of sense imagery.

Comparatively rare is the third type of "thought-rhythm," the balanced or parallel form. The best example of it is the "Onondaga Lament," as recorded in the Iroquois *Book of Rites*:[37]

Haihhaih!	Woe! Woe!	Woe! Woe!
Jiyathontek!	Hearken ye!	The clear places are
Niyonkha!	We are diminished!	deserted.
Haihhaih!	Woe! Woe!	Woe!
Tejoskawayenton.	The cleared land has become a thicket.	They are in their graves— They who established it— Woe! The Great League.

. . . .

The fourth pattern is the interlacing "thought-rhythm," skillfully done in the continuous song in "The Hako" which Fletcher subdivides as "The Morning Star" and "The New Born Dawn." Both are her translations from this Pawnee ritual. In "The Morning Star,"[38] repetitions occur in both the first and third stanzas, and the second and the fourth stanzas, which I have italicized for clarity:

I

Oh, Morning Star, for thee we watch!
Dimly comes thy light from distant skies;
We see thee, then lost art thou.
Morning Star, thou bringest life to us.

II

Oh, Morning Star, thy form we see!
Clad in shining garments dost thou come,
Thy plume touched with rosy light.
Morning Star, thou now art vanishing.

The New-Born Dawn[39]

III

Oh, youthful Dawn, for thee we watch!
Dimly comes thy light from distant skies;
We see thee, then lost art thou.
Youthful Dawn, thou bringest life to us.

IV

Oh, youthful Dawn, we see thee come!
Brighter grows thy glowing light
As near, nearer thou dost come.
Youthful Dawn, thou now art vanishing.

This pattern of interlacing design of "thought-rhythm" is the most graceful and most difficult form. It is used for narrative and descriptive purposes.

In summarizing the result of her research, Professor Barnes concludes: "On the whole, Indian lyric poetry is highly rhythmical in structure, although not closely metrical."[40]

VII *More Construction Peculiarities*

Several other peculiarities of construction exist in Indian verse. Most stanzas are from 3 to 6 lines in length, though some contain 100 lines, as in the case of the "Prayer of the First Dancers" in the Navajo "Night Chant." This variation in length of lyric and ritual verses is because the ceremonials could continue for days. Since all Indian poetic expression was oral, certain demands were made on the poet to mark off stanzas. He tended to drop his musical pitch at the end of each verse paragraph, or he completely changed his rhythm to mark a distinct change in thought from one stanza to the next. Another distinguishing mark of Indian verse is the great elasticity in the length of the line, which may contain anything from a single word to a whole sentence.

An illustration of a one-line song expressed in a single sentence is the Nez Perce "Scalp Dance." According to Herbert J. Spinden, "a night-time variety of the Scalp dance was invented by a man named Tukliks and was called *Tsū'huĭkt*. He was the only dancer, but others formed a circle about him and served as chorus. One of the songs was—'The scalps of people came to my mountains long ago.' "[41] Spinden described the dance as "the most important intertribal ceremony among the tribes" of the Columbia River plains in early days. It was a "triumphal celebration over trophies of war taken from the common enemies of the several associated tribes" of the Columbia Basin.[42]

After the Nez Perce gave up the custom of scalping enemies, their important tribal ritual took place in winter and was concerned with their animistic religious beliefs. Among the Nez Perce, dreams or visions induced by revery, fasting, and vigil were regarded as a "means of communication between the material world and the spiritual world."[43] These visions formed the most important factors in their religious beliefs. For this reason, the Winter or Guardian Spirit dance was the Nez Perce' dominant ceremony. Its central theme was the acquisition of a fresh vision or the renewal of an old one by an adult or child. In either case—of a new or renewal vision—the ceremony was supposed to bring the people, the animals, and other natural objects into close and friendly relationships.[44] Moreover, the Winter Spirit dance demonstrated to the villagers that the individual had succeeded in acquiring supernatural power. Men, women, and children participated in singing inherited songs or the ones they had obtained during the sacred vigil when each votary had gone to an isolated place to fast and pray for spiritual power and guidance. During the Winter Spirit ceremony, the singer started his or her song and danced alone; then other dancers took up the words—many times cryptic in meaning—and joined in the singing. No musical instruments were employed in the Winter Spirit dance; the singer mimicked whatever animal was mentioned. One eight-line song to a wolf repeated, "the wolf comes" in slightly varying ways. The first line, "Waila yawixne," was repeated three times in the eight lines.[45] Many songs and chants among the various tribes were not only sung, with or without words, but danced without any kind of musical accompaniment.

VIII   *A Rare Epic Poem*

While the Indian's poetic expression tends toward lyric and narrative poetry, only one example of an epic poem is extant. *Walam Olum*, the *Red Score* of the Lenni Lenape or Delaware

Indians, consists of a number of birch-bark plates which are incised and painted red. The pictographic record and a translation from the Delawares was obtained by Professor Constantine Samuel Rafinesque and first printed by him in 1836 in a work entitled *The American Nations*. Daniel Brinton,[46] an authority on Indian languages and editor of the *Library of Aboriginal American Literature*, determined the original words to be a genuine oral tradition written down by one not very familiar with the language. The epic is probably a traditional account of tribal movements from the St. Lawrence River to the Delaware.

The Lenni Lenape's history and customs had an unfortunate impact on their poetic thought. A brief discussion of their culture will increase understanding of the implications of the *Walam Olum*. The Delaware tribe of the Lenni Lenape confederacy was once the leading tribe of all the eastern Algonquians. Their territory included New Jersey, eastern Pennsylvania, lower New York, and vicinity. They had a tradition of peaceful relations with early white settlers, including the Quakers. A noted chief, Tamanend, who negotiated with William Penn in 1683, and whom the English called "Tammany," had his name immortalized in New York's political "Tammany Hall." When President George Washington sponsored the first Indian student at Princeton in 1789, he was George White Eyes, a Delaware, who pursued a classical education.[47]

The Lenni Lenape (meaning "real men") lived in substantial log houses in villages surrounded by stockades. They hunted, fished, and cultivated maize, beans, pumpkins, and tobacco. Like many other tribes, including the Nez Perce, they sought a vision quest for a guardian spirit, and they also had shamans who cured sickness. The Corn Dance and Gamwing were their important annual ceremonies. The Gamwing, held for two weeks in autumn, afforded men and women an opportunity to recite their visions, give names to children, and formalize adoptions. The Corn Dance in spring honored the Corn Mother. During it, the people recited a legend of how the corn came to the Delaware and how the Corn Mother protected all crops.[48]

Destruction of Lenni Lenape culture and tribal identity began in the 1700s when these peaceful tribesmen were exploited by the more aggressive Iroquois. Many Delawares migrated west-

ward to the upper Ohio where they sided with the French during
the French and Indian War. Others wandered northward to settle
in Ontario. After a series of westward movements, they reached
Indian Territory in 1867, and incorporated with the Cherokee.
Another group of homeless Delaware affiliated with the Caddo
and Wichita in western Oklahoma.[49] The Delaware and their
Algonquian family tribesmen gave many words to the English
language. Some of the more familiar are *wigwam, tomato, wampum, toboggan, moccasin, pow-wow, totem, squaw, papoose,
sachem, sagamore, tamarack, hickory, pecan, persimmon, hominy,
succotash, pemmican, squash, caribou, moose, opossum, rac-
coon, skunk, chipmunk, muskellunge,* and *terrapin.*[50]

One early writer has stated that this once admirable, proud
nation was reduced from 50,000 to 770 persons in 1886.[51] It is
small wonder that little remains of their poetry. A fragment from
the *Walam Olum* is quoted here as an example of the saga element in Indian song literature. This selection is an excerpt from
the third of the eight extant sections of the *Red Score,* often
considered the most poetic portion.[52] Daniel Brinton's synopsis
of this part clarifies certain vague phrases:

The waters [of the Flood] having disappeared, the home of the tribe
is described as in a cold northern clime. This they concluded to
leave in search of warmer lands. Having divided their people into
a warrior, and a peaceful class, they journeyed southward, toward
what is called the "Snake land." They approached this land in winter,
over a frozen river. Their number was large, but all had not joined
in the expedition with equal willingness, their members at the west
preferring their ancient seats in the north to the uncertainty of southern conquests. They, however, finally united with the other bands, and
they all moved south to the land of spruce pines.[53]

Brinton's comments about the narration, origin and prosody of
the *Walam Olum* are also of interest:

The narrator was probably one of the native chiefs or priests, who had
spent his life in the Ohio and Indiana towns of the Lenape, and who,
though with some knowledge of Christian instruction, preferred the
pagan rites, legends and myths of his ancestors. Probably certain
lines and passages were repeated in the archaic form in which they

had been handed down for generations. . . . Even to an ear not acquainted with the language, the chants of the "Walam Olum" are obviously in metrical arrangement. The rhythm is syllabic and accentual, with frequent effort to select homophones (to which the correct form of the words is occasionally sacrificed), and sometimes alliteration. Iteration is also called in aid, and the metrical scheme is varied in the different chants.[54]

Brinton's metrical transcription follows:

> After the rushing waters (had subsided)
> The Lenape of the Turtle [Turtle Clan] were close together,
> In hollow houses, living together there.
>
> It freezes where they abode, it snows where they abode,
> It storms where they abode, it is cold where they abode.
>
> At this northern place they speak favorably
> Of mild, cool (lands), with many deer and buffaloes.
>
> As they journeyed, some being strong, some rich,
> They separated into house-builders and hunters;
> The strongest, the most united, the purest, were the hunters.
>
> The hunters showed themselves at the north, at the east,
> at the south, at the west.
>
> In that ancient country, in that northern country,
> In that Turtle country, the best of Lenape were the
> Turtle men.
>
> All the cabin fires of that land were disquieted,
> and all said to their priest, "Let us go."
>
> To the Snake land to the east they went forth,
> going away, earnestly grieving.
>
> Split asunder, weak, trembling, their land burned
> they went, torn and broken, to Snake Island.
>
> Those from the north being free, without care,
> went forth from the land of snow, in different directions.
>
> The fathers of the Bald Eagle and the White Wolf remain
> along the sea, rich in fish and mussels.
>
> Floating up the streams in their canoes,
> our fathers were rich, they were in the light,
> when they were at those islands.

Head Beaver and Big Bird said,
"Let us go to Snake Island," they said.

All say they will go along
to destroy all the land.

Those of the north agreed,
Those of the east agreed,
Over the water, the frozen sea,
They went to enjoy it.

On the wonderful, slippery water,
On the stone-hard water all went,
On the great Tidal Sea, the mussel-bearing sea.

Ten thousand at night,
All in one night,
To the Snake Island, to the east, at night,
They walk and walk, all of them.

The men from the north, the east, the south,
The Eagle clan, the Beaver clan, the Wolf clan,
The best men, the rich men, the head men,
Those with wives, those with daughters, those with dogs,

They all come, they tarry at the land of the spruce pines;
Those from the west come with hesitation,
Esteeming highly their old home at the Turtle land.

IX   *Summary of Style*

It is worth-while to quote Professor Barnes's summary of the characteristics of Native American poetry:

1. On the formal side, three factors are outstanding in Indian verse:
   a. Brilliant execution of other repetitional forms instead of a general use of rhyme as an aid to rhythm.
   b. Extensive use of sense imagery and the imagery of comparison.
   c. Extreme economy of expression.

2. Minor qualities of Indian verse are humor, pathos, satire. The predominantly intellectual quality is largely lacking.

3. The characteristic qualities are imaginative, aesthetic and emotional in type. Their aspects are concreteness, rhythm, beauty, compactness, sincerity. The last aspect is a notable expression of the great religious motive which is dominant in all forms of native verse.[55]

Miss Barnes also finds that the factors influencing Indian song literature are spiritual quality, observation of nature, imagination, symbolism, and sense of beauty. The distinguishing traits of style are monotony, repetition, conciseness, poetic diction, imagery, and musical quality. Among the minor aspects are vigor, onomatopoeia, and parallelism.

Barnes's investigations have led her to conclude that the essence of Indian poetry is aspiration, and that its symbolism reveals penetration of thought, effects conciseness, and gives strength and beauty to the aboriginal verse. Indian poesy has beauty in thought and image, graceful phrasing, and symmetry of form.

An example of aspiration expressed through symbolism and incorporating the dominant religious motif is found in "A Dreamer's Thanks for Food"[56] from the Nez Perce:

> The light be upon us who believe,
> Leader of all with Power given,
> The Gleam beckons clearly before us,
> Our beings are nourished by [the] Gleam.
> Within us grow the callings of Life,
> Rain—falling on our Mother's bosom
> Body building foods are produced,
> And in its partaking we find strength.
>
> Better [to] die as Light is seen
> Than live to pass out in Darkness,
> In Darkness.

X Geographical Influences

Other distinctive features of Indian verse depend on environment. Barnes believes that the poetry is more stately in the north and lighter and more graceful in the south. The difference is largely of subject matter. "The Eskimo sings of his cloud-breasted mountains; the Omaha, of winding streams where weeping willows dip their branches; the Navajo, of flaming butterflies among the corn,"[57] and the Kiowa sings his songs of longing "like the open prairie where there is only the sweep of the wind."[58] Sensuous beauty is most highly developed in the songs of the southwest, and this quality is well exemplified by the

Hopi "Katzina" lyrics. Barnes further believes that the Pueblo tribes, partly thanks to their established places of residence, have produced the greatest poetry.[59]

Mary Austin also believes that there is a correlation between geography and poetic achievement and style. Her theory is that poetic "rhythm-patterns" can sometimes be identified as to origin on the plain, in the desert, or in the woodlands because, "in general, the poetry of forest-dwellers is more lyric than the songs of mountain and mesa."[60] Alice Fletcher expresses the belief that the verse of the woods-dwelling Chippewa is easier for Europeans to sing than the poems of other tribes, particularly those of prairie tribes. According to Barnes, a geographical influence may also be seen in the long, even, monotonous lines of "The Hako," a ceremony of the Pawnee Indians, whose territory is the open, rolling plains:

Crossing the Prairie[61]

Looking o'er the prairie, naught our eyes discern there,
Wide the land stretches out before us;
Then we cry aloud to Mother Corn: "Doth thy pathway
    lie here?"
Heeding now our crying, while our eyes she opens,
Mother Corn moveth out before us
On the lonely prairie, where we see straight the
    pathway lies there!

My own investigations have failed to establish this theory of geographical influence as a rule. Moreover, modern anthropology does not recognize these differences as being due only to geographical influences, but rather to additional modifications of a social and cultural nature.

The chief features, then, of the style of Indian poetry are ideas frequently expressed through symbolism; repetition, and the use of various patterns of repetition, instead of rhyme, as an aid to rhythm; monotony of phrase (to the non-Indian); brevity of expression; rhythm; the use of the "recessional" movement in lyric types; the use of the forward movement in dramatic types; parallelism; the extensive use of sense imagery; and free-verse form.

CHAPTER 2

Alice Cunningham Fletcher (1838–1923)

ALICE Fletcher, an ethnologist, made a pioneer effort to introduce Indian poetry into American literature. Sometime before 1880 she originated a system of lending small sums to Indians for buying land and building houses. She lectured frequently on general archaeology at the Peabody Museum of American Archaeology and Ethnology at Harvard University in 1882. She was appointed special agent to the Omaha tribe in April, 1883, to secure allotments in severalty, and she completed the work in June the following year. Her contacts with the Omaha resulted in the 1884 publication of *The Wawan or Pipe Dances of the Omahas* as the *Sixteenth* and *Seventeenth Annual Reports* of the Peabody Museum. No songs in this pamphlet were translated.

She then commenced an extended study of Indian music and songs, in which she was ably assisted by the Omaha Indian ethnologist Francis La Flesche, a head chief's son, whose grandfather was a French trader. This ethnological collaboration continued until Fletcher's death. When she became an assistant at Harvard to Professor F. W. Putnam in 1886, he encouraged her to work in archaeology and ethnology. To his early encouragement she attributed her "almost life-long interest in American Indian ethnology."[1] To insure the continuation of her Indian studies at the Peabody Museum, the Mary Copley Thaw fellowship was created for her in 1891 and continued until she died.

Fletcher's personal influence with Indians enabled her to add archaeological treasures such as the Omaha Sacred Tent of War to the museum's collection. Many of the results of her investigations among the Sioux, Winnebago, Omaha, Pawnee, and other tribes were published in the reports and papers of that institution, including "A Study of Omaha Indian Music" (1893) coauthored

with Francis La Flesche "after ten years of study on the subject."
In addition, she received international recognition that year when
she presented a paper on American Indian music at Chicago's
International Anthropological Congress. Her "Love Songs among
the Omaha Indians" was published in the *Memoirs* of the Inter-
national Congress of Anthropology in Chicago in 1894. George
Cronyn's anthology, *The Path on the Rainbow* (1918), contains
ninety-six of her Indian poems, including those from "The Hako."
Representative selections of her translations also appear in
Professor Day's volume, *The Sky Clears* (1964).

I *Significant Contributions*

One of Fletcher's important contributions to ethnology is
"The Omaha Tribe," which appeared in the *Twenty-Seventh
Annual Report* of the Bureau of American Ethnology in 1911.
This work has been called "an authoritative, monumental study
of its subject, the result of many years of research, and written
in collaboration with her adopted son, Francis La Flesche."[2]
Fletcher's devoted interest in Indian music is believed to have
stemmed from her severe attack of inflammatory rheumatism
while she was living among the Indians, a disease which crippled
her for life. The Indians were so solicitous about her illness that
they came daily to her bedside to sing her back to health. She
remembered the songs and upon her recovery wrote them down.

Another of her principal works is her transcription of "The
Hako," a Pawnee ceremony composed of twenty rituals and two
additional ones incidental to the main rites, all of which she
renders in the rhythms of the original. Her translation was based
upon the symbolism of the accompanying ritual acts that were
unequivocally explained to her by the Chaui band of Pawnee.
The transcription is the first complete record of the ritual and
music of a Plains Indian religious ceremony. This sharing by
the Indians of their cultural heritage with Fletcher was a rare
tribute that betokened their esteem for a friendly white woman.
In view of "The Hako"'s unique qualities of revealing esoteric
mysteries, this ceremony is the prime object of critical examination in this chapter.

The Pawnees were a semi-nomadic, buffalo-hunting plains confederation of Caddoan peoples that were related linguistically to the Wichita, Caddo, Arikaree, and several other tribes. In frontier times, the Pawnee roamed over the rolling hills and the grass-covered prairies of southern Nebraska and northern Kansas. Some authorities believe the tribe originated in the southwest, possibly even in Mexico; and Pawnee mythology and traditions seem to lend weight to this theory. Certainly, their hauntingly beautiful creation myth involving the gods Morning Star and Evening Star and the ancient rites connected with the myth are curiously similar to the human sacrifices of the pre-Columbian Aztecs in the Valley of Mexico. The Skidi (Wolf) Pawnee rites culminated in a human sacrifice at the time of the summer solstice. Legend claims that Petalesharo, the hereditary young Skidi chief, stopped the gruesome practice when he rescued a Comanche girl, the intended victim, probably in the 1820s. He defied the priests by forbidding any more human sacrifices.[3]

The Pawnee, unlike most of the plains nomads, abided in conical, earth-lodge villages near their fields where they culti-vated corn, beans, pumpkins, and squash. Their lives were regimented by ritual. The entrance to their lodges had to face the rising sun. The round, domed roof, made by a framework of poles covered with earth, symbolized the sky. Each post represented a star, and each was connected with some divine being. Thus, much of "The Hako" ritual relates to the earth lodges.

II   Summary of "The Hako"

The ritual drama of "The Hako" has been likened to a Medieval miracle play, for the ceremony

emphasized, on the one hand, man's dependence on the supernatural for all the gifts of life, and on the other hand, his dependence on the family tie for the gifts of peace and happiness. The specific teach-ings were reserved for the Son [one of the persons in the play]. These began in the ritual to the Dawn (tenth ritual) on the morning of the second and third days, which prefigured the secret ceremonies of the fifth morning, when the bond of the family relation was extended beyond blood kinship through the symbolic rites which recognized the common source of life in Tira'wa atius [the Master of Life, or the Supreme Being].[4]

The ceremony had a twofold purpose: to bring to certain individuals the "promise of children, long life, and plenty" and to insure friendship and peace for the participants and others who belonged to different family clans or tribes.[5] The song cycle was composed of ninety-five separate songs and nine incidental ones to the main rites. Following a period of preparatory rites, the ceremony's performance required five days and nights, which might also include a procession over the prairie from one village to another. This ceremony was held in the summer whenever someone wished to honor a member of another tribe or of another clan within his own tribe.

The chief persons in the drama were the Father, the Son, the Children, and attendant deities of Tira'wa atius, "the mighty power." Since man could neither see nor feel Tira'wa, lesser powers—the givers of breath, food, drink, fire—were created to mediate between man and Tira'wa. These mediators were considered the associates and representatives of the Master of Life.[6] Equally important in the ritual were Mother Corn, Kawas, the Eagle, the Morning Star, the Dawn, the Day, and Father Sun. The Father was chosen from the tribe which presented the spectacle; the Son—the person to be honored and leader of a group of children—was selected by the priests from another tribe by a curious process described in the Second Ritual. Unusual blessings were supposed to accrue to those who took the leading parts.

III *Beginning Rites of "The Hako"*

Because of their historical, religious, and mythological significance, certain phases of the prescribed ceremonial rites should be described. The initial rites included the First Ritual of "Invoking the Powers": preparing the feathered stems; painting the ear of corn; making other sacred objects; and offering of smoke. The actual ceremony began under the supervision of a man called the Ku'rahus (meaning a man of years, venerated for his knowledge and experience) who had been taught the sacred songs and instructed in their meaning. The man who sponsored the ceremony selected the Ku'rahus and set the day when the preliminary rites were to be performed.

On that day the Ku'rahus purified himself in the sweat lodge, then placed sweet grass on a pile of coals. Squatting on his heels, he drew a robe about himself and the coals so that the sweet grass smoke might reach every part of his body. After the purification, he took a bit of deer or buffalo fat consecrated to Tira'wa, mixed it with red paint, and anointed himself. Then, after putting on leggings and moccasins and tying a buffalo robe around his waist with the animal's hair rope, he fastened a white, downy, eagle feather in his scalp lock. Thus properly attired, and accompanied by his assistant and a novice, he went to the lodge of the man who had inaugurated the ceremony.

An assemblage of chiefs and leading men gathered at the lodge. The Ku'rahus sat at the lodge's west end, facing east. Spread before him on a mat were the materials to be used in the ceremony. After the Ku'rahus began singing the songs appropriate to the act of preparing the holy articles, everyone present had to remain seated in place. If there was any deviation or omission in the sequence of the rites, their purpose would be nullified.[7]

The first thing to be made was the feathered stem carried by the Ku'rahus. It represented the female element and led in the ceremony because the Pawnee believed that life first took form through the female. The stem was painted blue, which symbolized the sky, the dwelling place of the powers; and the paint was made from blue clay mixed with running water, which symbolized the continuation of life through successive generations. Another feathered stem, carried by the Ku'rahus's assistant, represented the male principle; it was painted green to symbolize Toharu, the vegetation which covered Mother Earth, and was a gift from Tira'wa, the power above. A fan-shaped pendant made of seven feathers from a young brown eagle (called a white eagle by the Ku'rahus), was hung upon the green stem. Warriors wore eagle feathers, and the bird was considered the war eagle—fighter, defender, and protector. Thus, male and female forces were combined on the sacred feathered stems.[8]

In "Invoking the Powers" in the First Ritual, an appeal was made for the lesser powers to intercede with Tira'wa, "the father of all," for help. This opening song, Fletcher stated, foreshadowed the movement and the purpose of the entire ceremony. Both words and music reached a climax in the third "phrase," she explained, because each third line directly invoked one of the powers or deities. The six stanzas belonging to the first part suggest six symbolic "motions" indicating the four cardinal directions, the above, and the below. The second part of the song sequence is in seven stanzas. The number suggests seven symbolic motions that indicate the same directions as those in the first part and, in addition, the center or the ego. Thus, the first part symbolizes the creation of physical life, and the second part recognizes psychical life. Since thirteen stanzas comprise the opening song but since the first, second, and fourth lines are repetitious, only the third line which is not repetitious is quoted in each of the remaining twelve stanzas. The first stanza is as follows:

> We heed as unto thee we call;
> Oh, send us thy potent aid!
> Help us, oh, holy place above!
> We heed as unto thee we call.

The order in which the powers are addressed in stanzas I–VI reveals something of the Pawnee idea of man's relationship to the supernatural. First to be invoked is the "holy place," the abode of Tira'wa, the father of all, who is not directly addressed. Instead, a definite locality is mentioned to fix man's mind on where prayer should be sent and from where help might come.

II

[Repeat first, second and fourth lines from above.]

Help us, Hotoru, giver of breath!
(Hotoru is the invisible Wind, the bearer or giver of breath.)

III

Help us, Shakuru, father of strength!
(Shakuru, the Sun, is the "father of strength.")

IV

Help us, h'Uraru, mother of all!
(H'Uraru, the Earth, is the mother, the conserver of life.)

V

Help us, Toharu, giver of food!
(Toharu, or Vegetation, is the "giver of food.")

VI

Help us, Chaharu, giver of drink!
(Chaharu, Water, furnishes life-giving liquid to man. Thus,
these lesser powers bring the gifts of life to man.)

VII

Help us, Kusharu, sacred to rites!

This first stanza of the second part calls on people to pay heed
to Kusharu, the place reserved for sacred purposes whence
man's thoughts could ascend to the powers that gave him life.
Fixing of a sacred place made a center from which daily life
could be set in order. It also made the inauguration of rites possible—the rites that served as a common bond to hold the community together.

VIII

Help us, h'Akaru, abode of life!
(H'Akaru conveys the idea of a place where life [h', breath] can
be received.)

IX

Help us, Keharu, wall of defense!
(Keharu refers to the actual dwelling to be erected for
protecting life.)

Keharu apparently corresponds to the male element represented in the first part by the Sun, the father, the giver of
strength. Throughout this ceremony, the position of the feathered
stem, representing the male, is upon the outside, where it acts
as guard and protector, a wall of defense to the interior of
the lodge which with its fireplace represents the nest.

X

Help us, Kataharu, center within!
(Kataharu, the fireplace, is the center where life within the
lodge is conserved; it represents the female principle.)

XI

Help us, Kekaru, promise of fire!
(Kekaru, the glowing coals, is a promise of the fire to follow.)

XII

Help us, Koritu, word of the fire!
(Koritu, the flames, the "word of the fire" refers directly to making fire by friction. This ceremony seems to underlie most, if not all, aboriginal rites through which man appeals to the powers for the means of sustaining life, as in stanzas V and VI.)

XIII

Help us, Hiwaturu, emblem of days!
(Hiwaturu, the "emblem," is the passageway representing the ego, the path wherein man passes to and fro as he lives his individual and communal life.)[9]

IV *Symbolical Meanings in "The Hako"*

"The Hako," named for the sacred and symbolical articles used in the ritual, illustrates all the qualities of Indian versification as they have already been summarized by Professor Barnes. Its theme is of cosmic dimensions, recounting the spiritual quest for the continuation of life. The concrete imagery ranges from the constellations, the sun, the moon, night and day, to the winds, trees, rivers, mountains, mesas and prairies, the earth, the life-giving corn, and the birds.

Besides these qualities, the "Chant to the Sun"[10] expresses aspiration:

> Now behold; hither comes the ray of our father
> Sun; it cometh over all the land, passeth in
> the lodge, us to touch, and give us strength.

Such aspiration is also true of the "Song to the Pleiades":[11]

> Look as they rise, up rise
> Over the line where sky meets the earth;
> Pleiades!
> Lo! They ascending, come to guide us,
> Leading us safely, keeping us one;
> Pleiades,
> Us teach to be, like you, united.

The "Chant to the Sun" is the first of four verses in the Eleventh Ritual, sung on the second ceremonial day. The Pawnee believe that "whoever is touched by the first rays of the sun in the morning receives new life and strength" because the rays have been brought directly from Tira'wa atius. The sun's first rays "are like a young man, they have not yet spent their force or grown old, so to be touched by them is to receive an accession of strength."[12] The singers petition for success in hunting and in war, for plenty of food, and for children and health. These verses are chanted as the first ray enters the door of the lodge bringing the promise of strength and power to all within. The chanters then pause until afternoon when they sing four more songs to accompany the ray as it leaves the lodge, touches the hills, and sinks with the sun in the west, leaving the land in shadow.

The Twelfth Ritual, sung on the second ceremonial night, contains the invocation to the Pleiades in the third song of the cycle. This poem and also the "The New-Born Dawn" (quoted previously) are good examples of the Indian's imagery of comparison, for the Pleiades is symbolically likened to a guiding, unifying principle needed to maintain tribal identity. The "youthful Dawn" is compared to a young man with the promise of bringing life to the people; this promise is realized in the last four verses of the "Chant to the Sun" in the Eleventh Ritual.

"The Song to the Trees and Streams,"[13] a part of the Fifth Ritual, is chanted by members of the Hako party during their journey to the lodge of a distant village wherein the Son resides. Since the purpose is sacred, the singers must address with song every object met along the way because Tira'wa, the mighty power, "is in all things. Everything we come to as we travel," says the Kurahus, "can give us help, and send help by us to the Children."[14] Trees and streams are among the lesser powers, and so they merit their own songs.

As translated by Fletcher, the imagery in this song shows a tendency toward impressionism, and there is a distinctly lyrical rhythm:

> Dark against the sky yonder distant line
> Lies before us. *Trees we see, long the line of trees,*
> Bending, swaying in the breeze.
>
> Bright with flashing light yonder distant line

Runs before us, *swiftly runs, swift the river runs,*
Winding, flowing o'er the land.

Hark. Oh, hark. A sound, yonder distant sound
Comes to greet us, *singing comes, soft the river's song,*
Rippling gently 'neath the trees (italics added).

The smooth, flowing rhythm is partly effected by variations in
the repetition of the second line of each stanza, as indicated by
the italics. This variety of repetition, found throughout the
poem, is simple: it is the iterative type, in which the repetitions reappear either at the opening or close of each stanza;
double, where the story-phrase and the burden or refrain are
repeated; and reduplicating, which consists in repeating the
syllable, as the stem, for emphasis, or the last syllable when it is
used to complete the measure.[15]

V   *Literal and Free Translations Compared*

How successful Fletcher has been in translating the rhythm
and verse forms might best be illustrated by a comparison of a
line in the native language with the literal and free translation.

> Line 1361: *Hiri! Riru tziraru; rasa ruxsa*
> *pakara'ra witz pari; hiri! tiruta; hiri! ti*
> *rakuse tararawa hut, tiri.*[16]

The literal translation reads:

hiri! harken!
riru tziraru, by reason of, by means of, because of. The word has a
wide significance and force throughout the ritual.
rasa, the man stood.
ruxsa, he said or did.
pakara'ra, a loud call or chant, sending the voice to a great distance.
Witz, from *tawitz'sa*, to reach or arrive.
pari, traveling. These five words tell of a religious rite performed by
the leader. The first two refer to his going to a solitary place to fast
and pray, seeking help and favor from the powers above; the last three
describe his voice, bearing his petition, traveling on and on, striving
to reach the abode of Tira'wa [the Great Spirit].

hiri! harken! a call for reverent attention.
ti'ruta, special or assigned places, referring to the places where the
lesser powers dwell, these having been assigned by *Tira'wa atius*, the
father of all.

hiri! harken! a call for reverent attention.
ti'rakuse, sitting; present tense, plural number.
tararawa'hut, the sky or heavens. It implies a circle, a great distance, and the dwelling place of the lesser powers, those which can come near to man and be seen or heard or felt by him.
tiri, above, up there, as if the locality were designated by pointing upward.[17]

The free translation is as follows:

Changing a Man's Name[18]

> Harken! And whence, think ye, was borne
>   Unto these men courage to dare,
>   Strength to endure hardship and war?
>   Mark well my words, as I reveal
>   How the gods help man's feebleness.
>   The Leader of these warriors was a man
>   Given to prayer. Oft he went forth
>   Seeking a place no one could find.
>   There would he stand, and lift his voice
>   Fraught with desire, that he might be
>   Invincible, a bulwark 'gainst all foes
>   Threat'ning his tribe, causing them fear.
>   Nighttime and day this cry sped on,
>   Traveling far, seeking to reach—
> Harken! Those places far above—
> Harken! Within the circle vast
>   Where sit the gods, watching o'er men.

    This song is one of the Incidental Rituals which concerns a custom common to all Native Americans—that of "changing the name in consequence of some new achievement. . . . If any man of the Son's party had achieved success in war and his achievements had been acknowledged by the people, he could request the Son to have the ceremony of changing his name performed."[19] The stanza reproduced here refers to the circle of the lesser powers who deliberate in council on the petition which made its way to them and gained their consent.
    In all her "Hako" translations, Fletcher tried to render the original rhythm in English yet present an interpretative version that would furnish connotations which might arise in the Indian

mind while the native listened to and watched the ceremony. She noted that

a rhythmic rendition which aims not only to convey the literal meaning but to embody the elucidations of the Ku'rahus [ceremonial leader] as well, has been made. Its words have been so chosen that the lines shall conform to the rhythm of the corresponding phrases of the song. This rendition is for the purpose of presenting to the eye and ear of the English reader the song as it appeals to the Pawnee who has been instructed in the rite.[20]

However, she encountered special difficulties in translating the song "Changing a Man's Name":

This dramatic poem is in a rhythmic form impossible to reproduce in English; neither is a literal translation adequate to convey its meaning, since a single word sometimes represents a complex action, to the understanding of which a knowledge of the customs and beliefs of the tribe is essential. The terseness of the expression was also intended to close the meaning to the uninitiated, keeping it sacred from the common people. Although the form of the . . . rhythmic rendition could not be determined as heretofore by musical phrases, the English version contains nothing which is not in the original text explained and amplified by the Ku'rahus.[21]

Fletcher noted that the rhythm of the drum always followed the emotion expressed in the song closely; and she likened it to a "great pulsating voice."[22] She found that in the

songs which accompany every ceremonial act . . . the thought to be expressed has determined the rhythm, which in turn, has controlled both words and music and fixed as well the time or duration of the notes. The unit of time is marked by pulsations of the voice or by drum beats, and the words are found bent by elisions or stretched by added vocables to make them conform to the musical measure.[23]

She further observed: "The variety of rhythmic forms in the songs of the rituals offers interesting material for the study of the relation of the musical phrase to the development of metrical language."[24]

VI *Summary of Ritual's Teaching and Promises*

Near the ceremony's end, the sixth song of the Fifteenth Ritual is sung while the participants are making sixteen circuits of the lodge, symbolic of completion. The two parts of the song sum up the rite's teaching and promises: they are the Ku'rahus's prayer for the ritual's fulfillment; they give "assurance that Tira'wa answered the prayer of man made through the 'Hako' ceremony";[25] and the song is a Pawnee affirmation of faith in a supernatural power for good:

> I know not if the voice of man can reach to the sky;
> I know not if the mighty one will hear as I pray;
> I know not if the gifts I ask will all granted be;
> I know not if the word of old we truly can hear;
> I know not what will come to pass in our future days;
> I hope that only good will come, my children, to you.

> II

> I now know that the voice of man can reach to the sky;
> I now know that the mighty one has heard as I prayed;
> I now know that the gifts I asked have all granted been;
> I now know that the word of old we truly have heard;
> I now know that Tira'wa harkens unto man's prayers;
> I know that only good has come, my children, to you.[26]

This song exemplifies several characteristic features of native poetic style; it employs a slightly varied pattern of repetition instead of rhyme to aid rhythm; it is a balanced parallel, free verse form; and it expresses aspiration. Pawnee ideals in the "Hako" ritual often demonstrate philosophic concepts, as it was partly a prayer for peace and a plea for the brotherhood of man.

VII *Omaha Myths and Rituals*

The Omaha were neighbors of the Pawnee. They were also farmer-hunters, who had formerly inhabited the west bank of the Missouri River in eastern Nebraska. The Omaha are a small tribe belonging to the Siouan linguistic stock. They probably migrated westward from the Appalachian Mountains. Their name is derived from the Indian word meaning "those who go against the current or upstream." The Omaha ceded their extensive hunting grounds to the federal government in a treaty signed on March 16, 1854, but they retained their farmlands as a reservation where they still reside in Nebraska.[27] They were more engaged in agricultural and industrial pursuits than in artistic expression.

Even so, Fletcher's governmental work among the Omaha resulted in her adapting their creation myths and their ritual chants for attending the sick. In rhythm, form, and imagery, the Omaha verse is typical Indian poetry, such as this free translation of the "Ritual of the Cosmic Forces":[28]

> Toward the coming of the sun
> There the people of every kind gathered,
> And great animals of every kind.
> Verily all gathered together, as well as people.
> Insects also of every description,
> Verily all gathered there together,
> By what means or manner we know not.
>
> Verily, one alone of all these was the greatest,
> Inspiring to all minds,
> The great white rock,
> Standing and reaching as high as the heavens
>   enwrapped in mist,
> Verily as high as the heavens.

Repetition is used here, as in "The Hako," to aid rhythm. The chant, of which the above quotation is but a small part, is imaginative, concrete, compact, and sincere.

The stanzas quoted form the opening ritual song of the Omaha Pebble society, whose members treated sickness. The song bears the marks of antiquity, Fletcher states, and she gives the following explanation of the Pebble society's teachings as told to her and Francis La Flesche by the old leader. This myth, she points out, may be a paraphrase of a ritual:

At the beginning all things were in the mind of Wakonda [the Supreme Power]. All creatures, including man, were spirits. They moved about in space between the earth and the stars (the heavens).

They were seeking a place where they could come into a bodily existence. They ascended to the sun, but the sun was not fitted for their abode. They moved on to the moon and found that it also was not good for their home. Then they descended to the earth. They saw it was covered with water. They floated through the air to the north, the east, the south and the west, and found no dry land. They were sorely grieved. Suddenly from the midst of the water up rose a great rock [the primal rock]. It burst into flames and the waters floated into the air in clouds. Dry land appeared; the grasses and the trees grew. The hosts of spirits descended and became flesh and blood. They fed on the seeds of the grasses and the fruits of the trees, and the land vibrated with their expressions of joy and gratitude to Wakonda, the maker of all things. . . .[29]

These rituals reveal how completely man is identified with nature in the mind of the Indian.[30]

VIII   *Her Poetic Contribution*

Walter Hough, in a critical evaluation of "The Hako," states that it

evidences the closest study of creed, cult, and ritual, including the many songs of the ritual . . . and stands unrivalled by any [records of a Plains Indian ceremony] which have succeeded it. Here for the first time did any observer step behind the veil into the esoteric mysteries of an Indian ceremony and record those beliefs which are the most difficult to collect from the ultra-conservative old men who know.[31]

Fletcher's work among the Omaha is considered by some authorities as equally important a contribution to ethnology as the monograph done among the Pawnee. She was considered a "woman of lovable character who had proved herself the Indian's friend in practise [*sic*] as well as in theory, by her sympathetic kindness she won the confidence of the chiefs and leading medicine-men of the tribes among whom she worked."[33] For this reason, they permitted her to witness the most sacred ceremonies, and to record the sacred tribal songs that were usually concealed from white people.

Rated by Professor Day as one of the "best translators from a literary point of view,"[34] Alice Fletcher served a long and "distinguished career as a collector, arranger, and translator of Indian songs."[35] In fact, her many studies are an invaluable contribution to "knowledge of the inner spirit and beauty of the Indian's concepts,"[36] and she ranks among the highest as an interpreter of Native American heritage and culture.

CHAPTER 3

Frances Densmore (1867–1957)

ANOTHER pioneer in the field was Frances Densmore, a former piano teacher and church organist. She began studying Indian music in 1893 inspired by reading Fletcher. Using Alice Fletcher's material, Densmore began lecturing on native music in 1895. In 1901 she wrote down the first original songs of her collection, which came from a Sioux woman near Red Wing, Minnesota. While studying Filipino music at the St. Louis Exposition in 1904, Densmore also recorded a song composed by the once-feared Geronimo, the Apache chief, that had been published as "Geronimo's Song" in the *Indian School Journal* (April, 1906).

In 1907, she began doing extensive research in Indian music for the Bureau of American Ethnology. These studies included the song verse of the Chippewa (Ojibway), Teton-Sioux, Hidatsa, Mandan, Cheyenne, Arapaho, Choctaw, Apache, Menominee, Pueblos, Tules of Panama, Nootka, Quileute, Ute, Papago, Pawnee, Omaha, Yuma, and Yaqui tribes. All musical recordings and poetic translations were published in bulletin form, and most were field recorded with the aid of an Edison Home Phonograph in 1907 and a Columbia Graphophone in 1908. She used the Graphophone continually until 1940. More recently (1956–58), her investigations included the music of the Acoma, Isleta, Cochití, and Zuñi Pueblos, the Maidu Indian music of California, and Seminole music. For sixty-four years this productive woman, almost constantly traveling, carried on impressive research. As a result, she has been called "the best known collector of North American Indian songs."[1]

I *Ethnohistory of the Chippewa*

Densmore made her first field trip in 1905 to Grand Portage on the north shore of Lake Superior. She visited the White Earth

Reservation in Minnesota to observe the Chippewa. The Ojibway —the Indians' correct name was corrupted by the whites into the "Chippewa" by which they are generally known today—is one of the largest nations north of Mexico. They once occupied shores of both Lake Huron and Lake Superior, and extended as far westward as North Dakota. A branch of the Algonquian family, they now reside on reservations in Dakota, Minnesota, Wisconsin, Michigan, and Kansas.

The Chippewa originally inhabited a region of dense forests, numerous lakes and streams. They lived in rectangular, bark-covered houses in summer, and depended on dugouts or birch bark canoes for traveling the waterways to fish and to hunt caribou. During the cold winter months, the Chippewa found shelter in dome-shaped bark lodges. When lakes and rivers froze over, they traveled about on snowshoes. In the north woods of Wisconsin and Minnesota, they and their linguistic brethren (Ottawa, Menominee, Sauk (Sac) and Fox, Illinois, and Shawnee) also occasionally cultivated corn, beans, and squash. In addition, they collected maple sap for sugar, a variety of berries, and wild rice in season.

When Densmore visited these Indians at the White Earth Reservation again in 1907, she heard songs of the Midéwiwin (Grand Medicine Society) at Leech Lake Reservation. Financed by the Bureau of American Ethnology, she began recording music and songs with a phonograph at the Chippewa agencies at Onigum and at White Earth. After that experience she made repeated trips during her vacation periods to visit this nation at various reservations to continue collecting and preserving a large body of their songs and music.

Beginning in 1911, Densmore went to the Sisseton Reservation, South Dakota, to collect and record Teton Sioux music. For the next forty-three years (1911–54), she traveled widely in the Midwest, throughout the West, including British Columbia, and the American Southeast gathering the musical scores and chants of the Indian tribes in those disparate cultural areas. However, it is not within the scope of this monograph to analyze critically Densmore's extensive works except for her Chippewa music studies and songs and for a brief discussion of Papago healing songs.

Although all of her publications were valuable studies in the disciplines of ethnohistory and musicology, for the purposes of this monograph Densmore's most important contributions were "Chippewa Music," *Bulletin* 45 (Washington, D.C., 1910), and "Chippewa Music II," *Bulletin* 53 (Washington, D.C., 1913) since they contain the most literary translations of Indian songs. In Professor Barnes's opinion, Chippewa poetry lacks picturesqueness, but it is expressive of the cosmic impressions so peculiar to Indian verse. This lack of effectiveness is partly because the songs are deliberately kept concise and deceptively simple, and are intended to keep their sacred or symbolic meaning hidden. Indeed, the most striking feature of Chippewa verse is its extraordinary compactness, resulting in a loss of color or sensuous beauty.[2] *The Path on the Rainbow* (1918) contains sixty-three of Densmore's Indian poems, and many selections are likewise found in *The Sky Clears* (1951–64). In both anthologies Chippewa verse predominates, with sixty-seven Chippewa poems cited in the former volume (1934 edition) and sixty from other tribes; in *The Sky Clears* there are twenty-six Chippewa poems quoted and a lesser number from each of six culture areas of North America and Mexico.

II *Grand Medicine Society*

Densmore's *Bulletin* 45 (1910) contains a collection of the music and the poems of the Midéwiwin, Grand Medicine Society. Both men and women who belonged to the Midéwiwin held secret initiation rites. Although healing formed a part of the ceremonies, Densmore describes it as a

native religion of the Chippewa. It teaches that long life is coincident with goodness, and that evil inevitably reacts on the offender. Its chief aim is to secure health and long life to its adherents, and music forms an essential part of every means used to that end. . . . The element of propitiation is . . . absent from its teaching and practice. . . . "[3]

This absence is odd because propitiation of the spirits is almost a universal custom of Indian folklore.

Densmore continues: "The songs of the Midé represent the musical expression of religious ideas. The melody and the idea are the essential parts of a Midé song, the words being forced into conformation with the melody."[4] Meaningless syllables are customarily added either between parts of a word or between words to accomplish this conformation because melody was evidently considered more important than the words.[5]

The ideas expressed in Chippewa medicine songs are similar to those of other tribes, but they differ somewhat in form. The songs, sketched as ideographs on birch bark, are brief. The ideas usually refer to such sacred Midé symbols as shells or totemic animals. The signs recall the words to the singer's memory. Although Native Americans used visual imagery more extensively than sound imagery, an example of the latter type is found in this Midéwiwin medicine song:

> The sound is fading away.
> It is of five sounds.
> > Freedom.
> The sound is fading away.
> It is of five sounds.[6]

As the singer did not explain the sense of the poem to the translator, its meaning remains cryptic.

III *Metaphor, Simile, and Magic in Songs*

Occasionally Densmore's translations bring out figures of speech that in their suggestive power rank favorably with the best Imagist work:

> ### Song of Spring[7]
> As my eyes search the prairie,
> I feel the summer in the spring.

This charming song mirrors no visible signs of spring, although the poet "felt it in the air" with the promise of coming summer. As Densmore comments: "The melody is marked by simplicity and well reflects the mood of one who discerns the first signs of spring on the familiar prairie."[8]

No less delightful is the simile in this brief expression of a Chippewa "Love-Charm,"[9] also one of the Midé songs:

What are you saying to me?
I am arrayed like the roses
And beautiful as they.

Love charms are a popular form of magic among the Chippewa. Ironically, the Indian woman who told the poem to the translator was, according to Densmore, the ugliest and dirtiest of any tribal member contacted. Presumably the native woman was hopeful that the love charm would work its magic upon her! She was warned by the other women in the village not to reveal any more magical love charms after they learned what she had sung in a secret place in the forest to the white visitor.

IV *Minor Qualities in Songs*

Irony and humor are minor qualities in Indian verse, and for this reason are quite rare, but Densmore has made an excellent translation of the ironic "The Man Who Stayed Home":[10]

Although Jinwábe considers himself a man
His wife certainly takes all his attention.

This song was sung at the war dances before a foray. It "was intended to shame all who, without proper excuse, failed to join the warriors." Densmore describes it as a "taunting, mocking melody, different from any other war song for admirably expressing the idea contained in the words."[11]

She offers a grim illustration of satiric humor in the "Scalp Song":[12]

I wonder if she is humiliated
The Sioux woman that I cut off her head.

For two centuries the Chippewa's arch enemies were the Sioux (Dakota), also a large and powerful nation. The Chippewa early acquired firearms from white fur traders and after 1670, began driving the Sioux out of the woods and onto the plains. This "song of derision" was sung in a short, crisp rhythm on the return to the village of a victorious war party when all the participating warriors proclaimed their exploits at the celebratory victory dance. When a warrior returned bringing a scalp, all the men and women of his clan danced "around him with their arms full of presents, after which they distributed the presents throughout the village in his honor."[13] The songs were composed on the homeward journey in preparation for the occasion.[14]

V *Chippewa Love Songs*

Another song mixes irony with its humor:

> You desire vainly that I seek you,
> The reason is, I come to see
>   your younger sister.

The rhythm of this song is "smooth and flowing, the irregular divisions blending in an effective whole," according to Densmore. "The song is distinctly minor in tonality and freely melodic in structure."[15] Although Densmore describes Chippewa love songs as "plaintive in character, usually expressing sadness and disappointment,'[16] this sample indicates a lover's fickleness instead.

The most interesting love song of the collection, in Densmore's opinion, is "My Love Has Departed"[17] which was told her by an aged Chippewa woman. This poem suggests a longing for a loved one who "has gone on before"—who has preceded the singer to death:

I

> A loon
> I thought it was
> But it was
> My love's splashing oar.

II

> To Sault Ste. Marie
> He has departed.
> My love
> Has gone on before me
> Never again
> Can I see him.

Densmore says that this song is an "example of a common form of Chippewa songs, in which the first and last parts are alike,

the middle section differing slightly and often being the only part
in which words occur. Like most of the love songs, it was sung
tempo rubato."[18]

VI   *Papago Healing Songs*

Densmore traveled to the Southwest in 1920 to study Papago
music; and among the Papago songs she collected were ones to
cure an injury caused by a horse. The following whimsical
protest, "You Tied Me with a Black Hair Rope,"[19] is one of four
songs that tell a story about a black horse who came from the
east, "half dead with hunger and thirst." He was taken to a
water hole by an Indian boy, but afterwards was treated badly.
The third song expresses the horse's viewpoint about his treatment:

> Black hair rope is what you used in roping me.
> You treated me badly.
>
> You even threw me down and tied me.
> Not satisfied with that, you tied a knot
>   in the end of my tail.
> That made me disgusted.

"The general character of this song is plaintive," Densmore
notes. She explains that the four songs "are attributed to a black
horse, which was heard singing them" by a dreaming man. The
songs "were sung [by a medicine man] to cure [a patient of]
an injury caused by a fractious horse. As in other healing songs
the remedy was provided by the cause of the difficulty."[20]

The Papago respected animals as superior beings who were
better adapted to their environment than man. Animals gave
power (to people), but they also sent disease to humans who
wantonly killed animals when they didn't need food. The Papago
believed that by describing a desired event in magical, beautiful
speech, they could make that event take place. Hence a specialist
who sang the correct magical healing song could cure a patient.
One such poem, translated by Ruth Underhill, provides a pleas-
ing contrast to Densmore's more literal translation, and also
demonstrates the Indian's keen observation with typical imagery:

The Eagle's Song[21]

The sun's rays
Lie along my wings
And stretch beyond their tips.

VII   *Peaceful Papagos*

The Papago dwelled on the Arizona desert south of what is now Tucson, and they have preserved the old ceremonies and games. During the winter, they lived in the desert hills near a spring; in the summer's "rain-moon," they moved down to the desert floor where they held ceremonies to "pull down the clouds" in order to summon the rain so vital to their life cycle of planting, harvesting, and gathering wild plants. Papago men drank fermented saguaro cactus juice as they sang, and the villagers, women included, danced for two nights to induce precipitation. After summer rains had moistened the earth, each family planted its field of corn. For many nights thereafter, the Papago farmer walked around his plot, "singing up the corn" with the appropriate song to encourage the growth of various stages of the plant. The Papago still inhabit their ancestral villages where they till their fields of corn, beans, and squash, raise stock, and hunt the small desert deer. In earlier times, they found self-expression in song, which offered solace from a harsh, primitive existence in an inhospitable wasteland. Song "was a magic which called upon the powers of Nature and constrained them to man's will. People sang in trouble, in danger, to cure the sick, to confound their enemies, and to make the crops grow."[22] Poets, not warriors, were honored in this peaceful tribe. This curious tradition of glorifying poets even extended to the warpath. The Papago went to war, not to seek glory but only to defend their lives and property against enemies. Once launched on a hostile mission, these farmer-warriors performed the owl-meeting ceremony. They believed that dead Papago inhabited owl bodies whenever they wished to revisit their old home. Since they could get news from almost anywhere, they could inform the warriors where their enemies could be ambushed. Should the medicine man who communed with such owls be wrong, his life could be forfeited.

After a battle, those who did not kill the enemy were honored upon the party's triumphant return to the village. Warriors who had slain a foe and lifted his or her scalp had to remain in seclusion and perform a purification ceremony of singing and dancing every evening for sixteen nights. "What of a society," asks Dr. Underhill, "which puts no premium whatever on aggressiveness and where the practical man is valued only if he is also a poet?"[23]

VIII *An Extensive Contribution*

All but the Papago poems in the chapter are taken from Densmore's Chippewa translations. As she is primarily a musician, as her Chippewa pieces are considered her best work, and as examples of other kinds of Chippewa songs are given for comparative purposes in the chapter on Alice Corbin Henderson, no further Densmore translations will be quoted here. The critics consider her the "best commentator upon Indian love songs" because of her extensive musical researches among "many widely scattered tribal groups." She is also a skillful translator and her "observations on the general subject of Indian poetry" are considered "highly authoritative."[24] She has probably collected more songs and recorded more music from a greater number of different tribes than any other researcher. Her numerous field studies, which she pursued until the age of eighty-seven, form a vast body of ethnomusicological knowledge about the North American Indians, most of which is preserved in the Smithsonian Institution, the National Archives and the Library of Congress. The Densmore Collection is a fitting monument to a dedicated scholar of Native American lore.[25]

CHAPTER 4

Mary Hunter Austin (1868–1934)

O NE of the most successful of modern poets to interpret the spirit of Indian songs and chants is Mary Austin, a novelist, playwright, and essayist who lived near and with Indians for many years in California's San Joaquin and Owens River valleys and in Santa Fé, New Mexico. In 1888, Mary Hunter, her mother, and her brother Jim, homesteaded land in the Tejon region of California's San Joaquin Valley. This move brought her into contact with the Paiute, Shoshone, and other Indians. The change was a fateful but fortunate one for Mary. Ten years earlier, she had been attending public schools in Carlinville, Illinois, when her father died. In 1884 she had entered Blackburn College in Carlinville. The next year, she enrolled in the State Normal School in Bloomington, Illinois, and three years later she received a diploma from Blackburn before moving to California.

A year after the family moved, Mary taught school at Mountain View, and on May 18, 1891, she married Stafford Wallace Austin, a vineyardist and the manager of an irrigation project in the Owens Valley on the fringe of the Mojave Desert. When the project failed, Mary's husband taught school at Lone Pine. In 1892, Mary gave birth to a daughter, Ruth, and had her first story about the desert environment's effects upon its inhabitants accepted by the *Overland Monthly* (San Francisco). Partly to augment the family income, she taught at the Academy in Bishop from 1895 to 1897, then transferred to a teaching job at Lone Pine where her husband became the county superintendent of schools the next year.

Mary's family life had become increasingly unhappy, so she went to Los Angeles in 1899 to teach at Normal School while her estranged husband became registrar of the land office at

Independence in the Owens Valley. She then met Charles F. Lummis, a well-known collector of Indian and Spanish folklore, who became instrumental in founding the Southwest Museum and who was editor-publisher of the *Land of Sunshine* magazine (November, 1894), which he renamed *Out West* in 1902. Between 1897 and 1904 he printed many of Mary's early stories and poems, thereby encouraging her literary efforts through his role as "friendly critic."

She returned to her husband in Independence in 1900. At that time she achieved personal success by selling stories to the *Atlantic Monthly, Cosmopolitan,* and *St. Nicholas* magazines. However, she was forced to place her eight-year-old daughter Ruth in a private institution for the mentally retarded at Santa Clara. The publication of *The Land of Little Rain* (1903), one of her best known books, firmly established Austin's career as a writer. After moving to Carmel, California, in 1904, she met such literary luminaries as Jack London, George Sterling, Harry Leon Wilson, Charles Warren Stoddard, Ambrose Bierce, John Muir, Edwin Markham, Ray Stannard Baker, Lincoln Steffens, and others. That year *The Basket Woman* (1904) was published, followed by her novel *Isidro* (1905). Family problems again plagued Mary in 1906 when she became permanently estranged from her husband, but another book, *The Flock,* came out. Both *Isidro* and *The Flock* are other works which have upgraded her diminished reputation today as a novelist and interpreter of Indian and Spanish people.

Austin traveled to Italy in 1908, the year *Santa Lucia* was printed in New York and London. A year later, when she went to England, she became intellectually stimulated by visiting the Herbert Hoovers and by meeting H. G. Wells, Hilaire Belloc, Bernard Shaw, Henry James, William Butler Yeats, and Joseph Conrad. Her *Lost Borders* appeared in 1909. She returned to Carmel in 1911 to continue writing books and producing plays. A year later she engaged in various feminist causes with Margaret Sanger, Anna Howard Shaw, Elizabeth Gurley Flynn, and others. Then in 1913 she joined the New York salon of Mabel Dodge, later Mrs. Tony Luhan of Taos, New Mexico. Stafford Austin divorced Mary on August 21, 1914, in San Bernardino, after which she undertook to handle eastern publicity for the Panama-

Pacific Exposition in 1915. While she lived and wrote alternately in New York and Carmel, California, her twenty-two-year-old daughter Ruth died in a mental institution, October 6, 1914. In 1922 Mary made a second trip to England and lectured before the Fabian Society, an association of socialists.

Austin became fascinated by Indian songs as far back as 1900 or earlier, and had been making a special study of them during most of her life. Since the province of this text is Indian poetry, only selections from her complete collection of poetry, *The American Rhythm* (1923, 1930, 1970), will be discussed. In addition to the "Amerindian songs re-expressed from the originals," the volume contains a penetrating essay that analyzes the Indian poetic impulse and presents a historical review of ancient European and Native American rhythms.

The 1930 revised edition, a heterogeneous miscellany of lyrics and chants, contains forty poems. Austin included poetry from most of the western tribes. Most poems were written by 1910 and published by 1914 in such national magazines as *Harper's Weekly, The Bookman, McClure's, Everybody's, Poetry, The Dial, The Forum, The Double Dealer, Harper's,* and *The Quill.*

Austin's earliest, and some of her less literary interpretations in terms of indigenous stylistic traits, had been obtained from bilingual Indian informants. She often read these poems to the original singer and tested them with drum beats.[1] According to her statement in the preface to *The American Rhythm,*[2] she was influenced by the works of outstanding ethnologist-translators like Fletcher, Densmore, Natalie Curtis, Daniel Brinton, Washington Matthews, and James Mooney. Some of their translations are reproduced in this text for comparisons with Austin's "re-expressed" interpretations.

In a letter to poet Witter Bynner, she described how she thoroughly saturated herself in the song's words, together with the background of place and circumstances, before she "gave forth the poem in the belief that it bore a genetic resemblance to the original."[3] At first she directed her "quest for primitive concepts, for folk-thought under folk-ways." In the beginning, because form interested her only slightly, she neglected to record the original form of the songs she collected. Instead, she stripped off the husk of the form to get at the kernel of experience. The use of rhythm as a medium for poetic drama began to intrigue her, and this interest apparently led to her intensive study of Native American rhythms.

Austin's volume opens with a delicate Paiute lyric, "Heart's Friend."[4] As interpreted by her, this poem illustrates the imagery of comparison done into an artistically balanced form:

> Fair is the white star of twilight
> And the sky clearer
> At the day's end;
> But she is fairer,
> And she is dearer,
> She, my heart's friend!

> Fair is the white star of twilight
> And the moon roving
> To the sky's end;
> But she is fairer,
> And she is dearer,
> She, my heart's friend!

In addition to her Introduction for *The Path on the Rainbow* (1918, 1934, 1962), eight of her Indian poems from the Iroquois, Yokut, Shoshone, Navajo, and Paiute tribes are printed in George Cronyn's anthology.

I *The Paiute*

During Austin's early homesteading days in the mountainous fringe of the Mojave desert, she came into contact with the Paiute, who ranged widely throughout the western deserts from California, the Great Basin of Nevada, and Utah, to the Kaibab Plateau of northern Arizona. They lived mostly among sagebrush, rocky canyons, and lava-scarred wastelands where they hunted rabbits, reptiles, and even insects and seeds in their desperate search for sufficient food. Flimsy brush wickiups provided shelter and shade from the burning rays of the summer sun for their basket making. However, these "poor relations" of the Shoshonean family became adept at raiding the early California ranchos for horses.

Paiute tribal folklore included few myths that explain the

earth's, man's, or animals' creation; but legends or adventure tales abounded that served to entertain. The Indians sang about their dreams, and were best known for their prophet Wovoka who inspired the Ghost-Dance religion in 1889-90 in western Nevada, as well as a whole chain of Ghost Dance poems. The revivalist Ghost Dance cult is said to be "the most important source of vision-inspired songs."[5]

Though Austin did not seem to be inspired by these songs, a discussion of them serves to enrich the general understanding of this type of traditional Native American verse, and demonstrates a translation that contrasts to that of the interpretative lyric, "Heart's Friend." These short poems followed a similar pattern from tribe to tribe in being rigidly fixed in form and in featuring the repetition of lines. Here is a Nevada Paiute example.

The Whirlwind[6]

The whirlwind! The whirlwind!

The whirlwind! The whirlwind!

The snowy earth comes gliding,

The snowy earth comes gliding,

The snowy earth comes gliding,

The snowy earth comes gliding.

"This song," the translator James Mooney says, "may possibly refer to the doctrine of the new earth, here represented as white with snow, advancing swiftly, driven by a whirlwind."[7]

Wovoka, the religion's founder, was the son of Tavibo, himself a Paiute medicine man. After Tavibo's death in 1870, Wovoka was brought up by the David Wilson family, white ranchers in Mason Valley, Nevada. In 1889, Wovoka inspired new hope among the dispossessed, starving reservation Indians by claiming that God had told him that a new messiah would arise in the spring of 1891 and that the buffalo would return to a land of plenty if the tribesmen would give up the ways of the whites and return to their old lifestyle. Happiness, peace, and a resurrection of dead ancesters would follow; and these resurrected people would bring followers all the material things they desired. The new religion spread like a prairie fire among the western tribes. Unfortunately, this revival, accompanied by white misunderstanding of the dance as warlike (especially among the Sioux), culminated for the Sioux in the massacre by the Seventh Cavalry of Chief Big Foot's band of 200-300 Indians, mostly women and children, at Wounded Knee Creek, South Dakota, in December, 1890.

James Mooney, the prime authority on the Ghost Dance religion, relates that Wovoka had a dream-vision about 1887 or 1888 during a serious illness and believed he was

taken up to the other world. Here he saw God, with all the people who had died long ago engaged in their oldtime sports and occupations, all happy and forever young. It was a pleasant land and full of game. . . . God told him he must go back and tell his people they must be good and love one another, have no quarreling, and live in peace with the whites; that they must work, and not lie or steal; that they must put away all the old practices that savored of war; that if they faithfully obeyed his instructions they would at last be reunited with their friends in this other world, where there would be no more death or sickness or old age. He was then given the dance which he was commanded to bring back to his people. By performing this dance at intervals, for five consecutive days each time, they would secure this happiness to themselves and hasten the event. . . . He then returned to earth and began to preach as he was directed, convincing the people by exercising the wonderful powers that had been given him.[8]

Dr. Clement Meighan, another Ghost Dance authority, points out that revivalist cults are a "widespread cultural phenomenon" in nearly all the world's continents; that they follow a similar pattern of origin and growth; and that they are often characterized by a violent conflict situation.[9]

Commenting on the songs, James Mooney states:

The Ghost-dance songs are of the utmost importance in connection with the study of the messiah religion, as we find embodied in them much of the doctrine itself, with more of the special tribal mythologies, together with such innumerable references to old-time customs, ceremonies, and modes of life long since obsolete as make up a regular symposium of aboriginal thought and practice. There is no limit to the number of these songs, as every trance at every dance produces a new one, the trance subject after regaining consciousness embodying his experience in the spirit world in the form of a song, which is sung at the next dance and succeeding performances until superseded by other songs originating in the same way. Thus, a single dance may easily result in twenty or thirty new songs.[10]

II *The Remarkable Cherokee*

Austin's volume includes the rare "Magic Formulas" from the Cherokeè. Rare, inasmuch as that nation, one of the largest and most enlightened of the American Indian tribes, has preserved few of its songs, music, and legends in written form. These surviving formulas were collected and translated literally by ethnologist James Mooney, but four of them were reinterpreted by Austin with the aid of Leota Harris, a Cherokee woman versed in the lore of her tribe.

Originally the Cherokee (southeastern kindred of the Iroquoian family), were found by the first white colonists in the Allegheny Mountain fastnesses of eastern Tennessee, the western Carolinas, northern Georgia, and Alabama. The Cherokee, known as one of the four Civilized Tribes (the others being the Creek, Choctaw, and Chickasaw), practiced intensive agriculture. In early times, they lived in towns with palisades surrounding their curved-roof, rectangular houses covered with thatch or bark. Since their forested hill country abounded in rivers and creeks, they traveled about in dugout canoes.

The Cherokee developed a tribal clan and government system of a high order. Having progressed rapidly in the civilized arts of farming, weaving, and breeding stock, the Cherokee began compiling a written code of laws in English by 1808. Finally, by 1837, they adopted a constitution patterned after that of the United States; and they had abandoned their traditional clan system—a group of related households in which descent was traced usually through the maternal line. These remarkable Indians also built roads, schools, and churches; and they were publishing a weekly newspaper by 1828.

Although the Cherokee formerly observed elaborate planting and harvest rituals, the use of charms for healing the sick, or for working magic against witches, loved ones, and their enemies was the chief concern of their rites. These sacred charm chants were passed on orally for generations until the half-white Chief Sequoyah invented a Cherokee alphabet in the early nineteenth century. It enabled the shamans (medicine men) to preserve many formulas in writing, and these were collected by the ethnologist, James Mooney.

III *Translations and Re-expressions Compared*

A comparison of Mooney's literal translation of the formula "To Frighten a Storm" with Austin's re-expression shows how successful the interpretation is in the preservation of native thought, rhythm, and free-verse form. According to Mooney, the storm is on the track of the storm's wife like an elk in the rutting season. The shaman (or medicine man) tells the storm that his wife's tracks lead through "the tree tops on the lofty mountains" and that, by following her path, he (the storm) will be undisturbed. This chant is recited in order to divert a storm that threatens to injure the cornfields.

> Listen!
> O now you are coming in rut.
> Ha! I am exceedingly afraid of you,
> But yet you are only tracking your wife;
> Her footprints can be seen there directed upward
>   toward the heavens.
> I have pointed them out for you.
> Let your paths stretch out along the tree tops on
>   the lofty mountains
>   and you shall have them (the paths) lying down
>   without being disturbed.
> Let (your path) as you go along be where the waving
>   branches meet.
> Listen![11]

Austin's spirited and artistic reinterpretation preserves the thought and rhythmic free-verse pattern with less obscure symbolism:

> Formula for Turning Aside a Storm[12]:
> Here you come, He-wind,

In your rutting wrath
Trampling and tossing.
Truly, I fear you!
But it is not I you are tracking.
It is your mate, whose footprints
Flash in white riffles of leaves
Up the slope of the mountain.

.   .   .   .

There in the middle air
None shall disturb your mating.

Austin comments that she considers this formula as the most poetic in concept where the "Wisher" appears least and where the "Wish" is stressed.

Another example is well worth quoting. The formulas exhibit the Indian's poetic imagination expressed in symbols. The formula "To Separate Lovers," Mooney explains, is used by a jealous rival, either to separate lovers or a husband and wife. "Blue," which refers to the hawk, denotes that this color brings trouble with it; "white" in the second paragraph indicates that the man reciting the formula is happy. The phrase, "to spoil their souls," means to change their feeling toward each other; and the expression "we shall turn her soul over" refers to turning aside the woman's affections.

Yu! On high you repose, O Blue Hawk, there at the
        far distant lake.
The blue tobacco has come to be your recompense.
Now you have arisen at once and come down.
You have alighted midway between them where they
        two are standing.
You have spoiled their souls immediately;
They have at once become separated.

I am a white man; I stand at the sunrise.
The good sperm shall never allow any feeling of
        loneliness.
This white woman is of the Paint clan; she is
        called Wayi'.
We shall instantly turn her soul over.
We shall turn it over as we go toward the Sun Land.

I am a white man. Here where I stand it (her soul)
    has attached itself to mine.
Let her eyes in their sockets be forever watching
    (for me).
There is no loneliness where my body is.[13]

Austin's poetic rendition closely approximates the literal one in
content, although it is less cryptic and more rhythmical:

Formula for Separating Lovers[14]

Ah, you dweller of the high places,
Blue Hawk, trouble bringer, of the far distant lake,
The blue smoke of tobacco I offer you in recompense!

Ah, now you have arisen;
At once you have come down to me;
You have alighted mid-way between them,
Those two that I have named to you;
At once their souls you have bemused.
At once they have become separated.

I am a man whose soul is white-glowing,
I stand at the sunrise; in me
The fire-sperm shall be proof against desolation
    of spirit.

The succeeding two stanzas almost duplicate the wording of the
original translation. It is evident from the excerpts that in her
re-expressions, Austin has succeeded in her purpose of expressing
in free verse the formulas' poetic values of "folk-thought under
folk-ways."

IV   Iroquois Ode a Free Translation

Unlike Austin's other work, which is interpretative, the
"Memorial Ode of the Iroquois" is a "free translation" that is
in its style a typical product of Indian poetic expression. According to the note, Chief John Buck, hereditary Keeper of the
Wampum (tribal historian), composed it in 1884 upon the re-
moval of Chief Red Jacket's (Sagoyewatha) remains to a new
burial place. This Seneca chief and orator was distinguished by
wearing a British scarlet coat and a medal given him by General
George Washington after the Revolution, although he had

reluctantly fought against the rebelling colonists. He became an alcoholic after raging for years against all whites.

The "Great League" mentioned in the ode refers to the League of the Five Iroquois Nations in western New York, comprised of the Cayuga, Mohawk, Oneida, Onondaga, and Seneca, all of whom were canoe and village Indians of the Eastern woodlands and members of the Huron-Iroquoian linguistic stock. Legend credits the League with having been organized (the Mohawks say circa A.D. 1000 or 1100, whites place the date circa 1450) by "the saintly statesman Deganawidah (son of a virgin mother); assisted by the great and noble councilor Hiawatha, a Mohawk, to put an end to broils and wars between the Five Nations and to establish a universal peace based on harmony, justice, and a government of law."[15] After they had formed their confederacy, the Iroquois became "the most notable and powerful community among the native tribes of North America"[16] for three centuries.

Austin's rendering of Chief John Buck's 1884 version of this chant appears to be a variation of the original "Ancient Rites of the Condoling Council," translated by ethnologist Horatio Hale in "The Iroquois Book of Rites," *Library of Aboriginal American Literature*, No. II. The lengthy ritual was recited at the mourning ceremonies for a deceased chief. The circumstances of the Great League's founding and the names of chiefs who were founders are recalled throughout the 222 pages of the "Book of Rites," which is a statement of both political and religious faith.

Austin's "free translation" of the "Memorial Ode of the Iroquois," attributed to Chief John Buck follows:

> Now, listen, Ye who established the Great League,
> Now it has become old,
> Now there is nothing but wilderness.
>
> Ye are in your graves who established it.
> Ye have taken it with you and have placed it
>   under you,
> And there is nothing left but desert.
> There you have taken your great minds.
> That which you established, you have taken with you
> Ye have placed under your heads what ye have
>   established,
> The Great League.[17]

In comparison with Austin's rendition of the "Memorial Ode," the first stanza of the "Rites of the Condoling Council" as translated by Hale reads:

> Woe! Woe!
>
> Hearken ye!
> We are diminished!
>
> Woe! Woe!
> The cleared land has become a thicket.
> Woe! Woe!
> The clear places are deserted.
> Woe!
> They are in their graves—
> They who established it—
> Woe!
> The great League.
> Yet they declared
> It should endure—
> The great League.
> Woe!
> Their work has grown old.
> Woe!
> Thus we are become miserable.[18]

It would appear that Austin's "free translation" of the ode was used in the sense of a free restatement or "re-expression" of the original in the "Book of Rites." A refrain is appended to Chief John Buck's version in Professor Cronyn's anthology *The Path on the Rainbow* (32) which, with slight variation in the wording, duplicates Hale's translation of the first stanza that has been quoted. It seems unlikely that Chief John Buck would compose the ode instead of reciting the traditional chant of the Condoling Council at Red Jacket's reburial rites.

Iroquois song literature abounds in ritual verse. The two rituals translated by Horatio Hale were based on documents kept by surviving chiefs whose duty was to carry on their ancient ceremonies. More than a century before Hale's 1883 publication of "The Iroquois Book of Rites," white Protestant missionaries, using a Roman alphabet, had written the rituals in Onondaga and Canienga (Mohawk) dialects. In the "Canienga Book," speeches of representatives from the original three nations to join in the confederacy—Mohawk, Oneida, Cayuga, respectively—were directed to the later members—Onondaga and Seneca—whenever a chief of their nations was to be lamented. Conversely, the "Onondaga Book" preserves the chants recited by the Onondaga and Seneca whenever they mourned a chief of the original three nations. Interspersed among the long, set speeches in both rituals are prayers, hymns, and chants. These are introduced by a roll call of the League's member villages and by a list of the chieftains who formerly ruled it. Translator Hale describes the "Book of Rites" as

. . . sometimes called the "Book of the Condoling Council," [it] might properly enough be styled an Iroquois Veda. It comprises the speeches, songs, and other ceremonies, which, from the earliest period of the confederacy, have composed the proceedings of their council when a deceased chief is lamented and his successor is installed in office. The fundamental laws of the league, a list of their ancient towns, and the names of the chiefs who constituted their first council, chanted in a kind of litany, are also comprised in the collection.[19]

The Indian phrasing is much more authentic in Austin's version of the "Memorial Ode" than in her mediocre interpretation of "The Song of the Hills"[20] with its descriptive mood and its sing-song rhythm, for neither device is characteristic of native verse:

> This is the song of the Hills
> In the hour when they talk together,
> When the alpen glow dies down in the west
> and leaves the heavens tender.

The note states this poem is based on a Yokut song "of a man and a woman who might have loved." Some forty or fifty Yokut tribes, noted for a stylized Deer dance, lived in the San Joaquin Valley of California where Austin spent several years as a homesteader and schoolteacher.

V   *Re-expression and Translation from Navajo Compared*

However, in Austin's other interpretations she returned to Indian form and metrics as exemplified in the "Prayer to the

Mountain Spirit,"[21] in which she brings imagery through iterative repetition:

> Young Man, Chieftain,
> Reared within the Mountain,
> Lord of the Mountain,
> Hear a young man's prayer!
>
> Hear a prayer for cleanness,
> Keeper of the *he* rain,
> Drumming on the mountain,
>
> Lord of the she rain
> That restores the earth in newness;
> Keeper of the clean rain,
> Hear a prayer for wholeness.

To compare Austin's re-expression of this poem with the original translation (Washington Matthews's "Invocation to Dsilyi N'eyani") is intriguing. This religious ceremonial from the "Mountain Chant" enacts tribal myths, and these myths form a sequential key for interpolated songs of sequence. The songs are chanted by a medicine man or other singers as part of the curative rites for illness. According to the translator, as the supplicant addresses the ritual prayer to the deity, Dsilyi N'eyani, she holds in her hand "the offering sacred to him."

> Reared within the Mountains!
> Lord of the Mountains!
> Young Man!
> Chieftain!
> I have made your sacrifice.
> I have prepared a smoke for you.
> My feet restore thou for me.
> My legs restore thou for me.
> My body restore thou for me.
> My mind restore thou for me.
> My voice restore thou for me.
> Restore all for me in beauty.
> Make beautiful all that is before me.
> Make beautiful all that is behind me.
> Make beautiful my words.
> It is done in beauty.
> It is done in beauty. (Repeated four times.)[22]

While Austin has borrowed several lines from the original and has retained the rhythm, she has omitted the repetition and has changed the supplicant into a young man instead of a woman, but she has kept the meaning of a "prayer for wholeness." Additional comparisons of Matthews's Navajo translations with other interpretations are found in the chapter about the work of Eda Lou Walton.

VI *Essence of Pueblo Poetry Captured*

Upon moving to Santa Fé, New Mexico, in 1924, Mary Austin devoted the last ten years of her life to studying Pueblo Indian poetry and Spanish folk culture. There, as in Carmel-by-the-Sea, California, an artists' and writers' colony had developed. She found her true identity at last expressed in her volume *The Land of Journey's Ending* (1924), a collection of prose sketches of Arizona and New Mexico.

Austin's poems that deal with the Pueblo tribes seem to capture most happily the true flavor of Indian rhythms, verse forms, and imagery. For example, "Rain Songs from the Rio Grande Pueblos" has the symmetry of form, the repetition for rhythm, and the chanting musical quality peculiar to Indian poetry.

> Cloud priests,
> Whose hearts ascend through the spruce tree
> On the Mountains of the North,
> Pray for us!
>
> Cloud priests,
> Whose hearts ascend
> Through the pine of the West,
>
> Through the oak of the South,
> Through the aspen of the East,
>
> Through the high-branched cedar of the zenith,
>
> Through the low, dark cedar of the nadir,
>
> Pray for us![23]

The second of the four stanzas of Austin's "Thunder Dance at San Ildefonso"[24] is also a good example of the Indian's imagery of comparison:

Hear the thunder calling
With the voice of many villages,
With the sound of hollow drums,
With the roll of pebbled gourds
Like the swish of rushing rain.
Hoonah, hoonah,
The voice of the thunder
Calling on the clouds to bring the summer rain.

Austin witnessed in the Rio Grande pueblos several rainmaking ceremonies of which the songs she reproduced were fragments, but all of them were "more or less derivative one from the other."[25] The "Thunder Dance at San Ildefonso" is a Tewa song of sequence belonging to the ancient rite of invoking the gods for rain, a custom that had fallen into disuse but was revived in the 1930s. She compared the repetitious phrases and figures of speech in many Pueblo songs to "the frequency of Homer's 'wine-dark sea.' "[26]

As the Spanish name for these tribes implies ("pueblo" means "town"), the conquistadores found them dwelling in adobe huts in walled villages along the Rio Grande and other rivers in the arid country of present New Mexico and Arizona. The Pueblo, the oldest inhabitants of the region, had developed in pre-Columbian times the highest level of culture found north of the Valley of Mexico. They were skilled in agriculture and in building houses of more than one story, and produced loom-woven fabrics as well as decorated in color designs on pottery and basketry. Former Commissioner of Indian Affairs John Collier has stated that the Pueblo have a magnetic attraction for peoples worldwide who study "living archaeology"—arts, crafts, social, political, and economic organization of these ancient Indian societies, even their land-use problems of water and wind erosion—to gain insights into their psychology and "metapsychology" which attracted the Swiss psychologist and psychiatrist Carl Jung to Taos Pueblo.[27]

Above all, the pueblo dwellers excelled in creating a lengthy ritualism, often composed of archaic chants and songs of sequence to accompany tribal feasts, prayer, worship, or healing rites. This highly developed ritual verse, designed for religious, ceremonial, or magical power, was formal in style. It was usually sung or recited as song-prayer in connection with symbolic worship and certain physical rites by shamans, medicine men, and priests. Their functions were divided: the medicine man primarily cured disease and gave protection from evil spirits; the shaman was also a conjurer or exorcist whose authority entirely depended upon his individual ability; and the priests conducted the rituals, although in many tribes the shamans' and the priests' functions were combined.[28] The Pueblos were represented by eleven songs in Austin's 1930 edition of *The American Rhythm,* and this number indicated their attraction for her.

VII *Personal Songs*

Indian verse is seldom personal, but a personal song is an individual's own possession. No one else may sing it without permission—a kind of primitive copyright. The owner may bequeath it to his tribe after his death, or he may, during his lifetime, give it to a friend. In some cases, he may never reveal it to anyone but the Great Spirit. Austin states that the personal song expresses an individual's own philosophy or a consummate spiritual experience. Such a song is often sung preceding a battle or upon the approach of death. In the latter case, the singer's friends frequently gather around the dying man and sing it for him.[29] The "Personal Song of Daniel Red Eagle" (an Oglalla Sioux), interpreted by Austin, illustrates in this third and last stanza a typical Native American trait—the Indian wastes no words in his poetical expression:

> The fierce hawk of death,
> When will it strike.[30]

According to Frances Densmore, the Oglalla were a band of the Teton Sioux, one of seven principal divisions of the large Dakota or Siouan family. Among the western Teton Sioux she found a great variety of songs. A recent investigator, Dr. Harry Paige, points out that individual or "solo" songs are unique in structure. Many appear formless, fragmentary, even cryptic in meaning. Their subject matter may deal with anything that strikes the composer with emotional impact, as is exemplified in his translation of the death song of an old Teton Sioux woman. As she lay dying in a reservation hospital room, her fading vision gazed at hills, sun, and sky and she sang:

> This land is beautiful,
> O Sun, now for the last time
> Come greet me again.[31]

Extensive ritual ceremonials, curing-spell songs, hunting and war songs, Strong Heart songs that were intended to instill honor and courage in the members of the Strong Heart Society, and especially mystical revival songs of the Ghost Dance generally characterized Siouan poetic literature. However, Austin's Siouan interpretations include only short personal songs.

VIII *Pathos in Native Verse*

Like humor and irony, pathos is another quality rarely found in Indian poetry. Austin, however, interpreted a song in which pathos is expressed in a stoical way by a southern Shoshone woman who was abandoned by her tribe because she was too old to keep up with their migration. This desertion of the aged was a usual custom among wandering tribespeople; a similar song was recorded by Densmore from the Pima. The following quotation from Austin's work is the first of four stanzas:

> Alas, that I should die,
> That I should die now,
> I who know so much![32]

The aged woman's plaint was the only protest against such a death that Austin had encountered.

IX *Onomatopoeia and Mysticism*

For a simple but a nonetheless excellent illustration of onomatopoeia, Austin's interpretation of a Paiute "Cradle Song"[33] apparently contains the essence of the original rhythm:

> Coo .... ah .... coo .... !
> Little Dove,
>
> Coo .... ah ..... coo!

> The wind is rocking
> Thy nest in the pine bough,
> My arms are rocking
> Thy nest, little Dove.

Since the greater part of Indian poetry is concrete, it is unusual to find a poem with a philosophical concept, but Austin has included one poem in her volume which she affirms is a symbolic representation of mystical seeking rather than a love song. In the "Song of Seeking," the Chippewa bard was probably searching for the ideal complement to his soul:

> The dear of my soul
> I have lost it;
> That lost Other
> I am seeking;
> All night awake
> I am seeking.
> I shall leave no place unsearched till I find her.
> At day break,
> I seemed to see her,
> It was only
> The flash of a loon's wing on the water,
> It is not that Other whom my soul seeketh.[34]

X *Austin's Place as Interpreter and Theorist*

Mary Austin was a prolific producer of prose and poetry, but only her Indian verse in her volume *The American Rhythm* is relevant for a critical evaluation in these pages. This work's poetic contents demonstrate Austin's faithful adherence to essentially Indian subjects and to rhythm-patterns, in which, rather than seek for lyric quality, she sought instead a "full expression" of Indian's thought by saturating herself in the poem, in the life that produced it, and in the environment "that cradled that life ..."[35] until she felt capable of expressing the folk-thought. Her essay on a native American rhythm, in her volume by that title, introduced a poetic theory that was based upon her widespread studies of Native American verse. Although Professor Day dismisses Austin's essay as "an impressionistic and rhapsodic attempt to work out an esthetic for the Indian rhythmic arts,"[36] her

biographer, Professor Pearce, who made an in-depth study of all
her work, affirms that her introductory preface

did more than introduce a phrase to poetic theory drawn from the
example of American Indian verse. Mary Austin pioneered the
inquiry into esthetic principles based upon indigenous motifs in
American life, motifs based upon the European as well as the Indian
experience here. If one probes the sources of each of her books, he
discovers this partly anthropological and partly philosophic quest
as the deepest motivation behind them all.[37]

Briefly summarized, Dr. Pearce's analysis reveals the following
salient points of Austin's poetic theory: Greek and other early
Mediterranean peoples' ritual chants may have had qualities
in common with American Indian rites. By comparing children's
responses to those of primitive peoples, she found that impulse
and response develop with individual and group motor incentives
and result in rhythm. Imitations of the sounds and the movements that have been heard and seen are the first stages of poetic
response. Onomatopoetic cries, tones, and evocative words appear in nonsense verse and nursery rhymes as well as in primitive
fertility rites. She cited "the imitative words and measure" in both
a child's jingle "Blacksmith, Blacksmith" and a Navajo gambling
song. After recognition comes the identification (or second)
stage with an object in which the child or the primitive "estab-
lishes a relationship between himself and what he sees or feels."
The third stage of poetic response, arrived at in both primitive
and juvenile creative effort, is generalization about group senti-
ment. "She feels that this often ties in with mysticism about the
land and with communal activities, but she is speaking of the
most elementary" verse types. "Her analysis does not proceed to
the stage of introspection and subjectivism which penetrates
poetry at all advanced levels." She searched for the basic
response to image and movement. Motor responses condition
the stresses and releases which bring pleasure in rhythm, and she
cited the swing of man in the saddle and his pacing on foot
which establish motor impulses in the brain. Her references to
"the landscape line" presumably applied to cadenced verse which
she believed to be governed by motor impulses conditioned by
actions or emotions experienced in a particular region. She could

always tell, she averred, whether a new Indian song originated in the plains, the desert, the mountains, or at the seashore. In future, she hoped for a fusion of Anglo-American and Indian traditions in verse.[38]

Critical estimates of Austin's work, Dr. Pearce found, "range from highly laudatory to moderately captious."[39] V. F. Calverton stated that her theory of prosody was fresh and original, and that it had not been adequately appreciated. Charles Lummis, editor of *Out West* and author of many published books about southwest Indian and Spanish studies, said in his book review of Austin's novel *Isidro* (September, 1905): "The one structured warning every friendly critic must wish to give Mrs. Austin is to beware of abstruseness and preciosity."[40] Lummis published seven poems and four short stories of Austin's work as well as a five-part serial and a long article on the 1906 San Francisco earthquake. Had he lived and reviewed her poetic theory, he would undoubtedly have made the same criticism of it. Professor Dudley Gordon characterizes her as "a writer of great potentialities which might have been fulfilled had she heeded her mentor's sincere advice."[41] Lawrence Clark Powell, now retired as Dean of the School of Library Service, University of California, Los Angeles, believes that, after Mrs. Austin left California, she "became self-conscious as prophetess, grew crochety, and lost the simple gifts of her youth."[42]

But she remains one of the early pioneers who investigated the aesthetic principles underlying indigenous motifs of Indian poetry. Her years in Santa Fé seem to have greatly influenced her later and more mature study of the Indian's metrical compositions. The result is reflected in her poetic theory and in her re-expressed Pueblo poems.

CHAPTER 5

Natalie Curtis (Burlin) (1875–1921)

T HE most original, and certainly the most unusual, contribution to American Indian literature is Natalie Curtis's *The
Indians' Book*, the first edition of which was published in 1907.
The book is a treasury of Native American musical transcriptions,
art, myths, legends, and song-poems, all of which were field
recorded at the turn of the century. Curtis, who was primarily a
musician, had studied piano in the 1890s at the National Conservatory of Music in New York and in Europe. While visiting
her brother in Arizona prior to 1903, she became a student of
Indian lore and life and began assembling Indian songs, myths,
and music. Thereafter, she traveled extensively over plains and
deserts in the United States by train, wagon, and horseback.
During a period of years, she collected and organized her
materials with the Indians'—and President Theodore Roosevelt's
—help. The Indians called her "Tawa Mana" (Song Maid) and
warmly responded to her friendship.

Because missionaries and agents frowned upon her efforts to
preserve indigenous cultures which they considered to be ob-
structing their acculturation attempts, Curtis appealed to President Roosevelt for assistance. Aided by his enthusiastic cooperation, she was then permitted to visit the reservations without
hindrance. She gave full credit to her collaborators in the title
page of *The Indians' Book*: "The Indians are the authors of this
volume. The songs and stories are theirs; the drawings, cover-
design, and title-pages were made by them. The work of the
recorder has been but the collecting, editing, and arranging of
the Indians' contributions." The year before the book appeared
under Harper's imprint, Curtis received a handwritten note from
the White House, signed by Theodore Roosevelt, and dated
"May 17th, 1906," which stated: "These songs cast a wholly new
light on the depth and dignity of Indian thought, the simple

beauty and strange charm—the charm of a vanished elder world—
of Indian poetry."[1] In addition to *The Indians' Book,* Curtis's
output of native songs and music after 1903 appeared in a host
of technical and national periodicals, including *Harper's Magazine, The Craftsman, Southern Workman, Dial, Craftsman Magazine, Musical Quarterly, The Nation, The Outlook, The Etude,
Journal of Art and Archaeology,* and *The Freeman.* She privately
published *Songs of Ancient America* in 1905, and lectured before
educational institutions and scientific bodies.

I *Indian Book Unique*

Most relevant to this study is *The Indians' Book* (1907), for
it not only contained 150 Indian poems but also served as a
source book for North American indigenous culture. Represented
are the eastern forest-dwellers; the plains and lake tribesmen;
northwestern coast inhabitants; and the southwestern desert
peoples. Curtis's arrangement of *The Indians' Book* is admirable.
An explanation of the myths, legends, folk and animal tales, customs, and traditions of each tribe is followed by the songs and
melodies that are an integral part of tribal lore. These notes make
the poems intelligible to non-Indian readers. The songs are
presented in the original language and in free translations, and
they are accompanied by musical scores. Many poems are traditional, but their origins have been lost. A few are from their
composers' lips; others are from the ancient lore keepers—the
oldest men—who sang the songs or recited myths and legends
in sometimes archaic language. Eleven of these poems are
represented in the Cronyn anthology and about an equal number
of them are reprinted in the Day collection. Although Curtis had
intended to extend and amplify her work, the project was never
carried out because of her untimely death in 1921.[2] Nonetheless,
The Indians' Book as it stands in either the original 1907 edition
or in the reprint editions of 1923, 1935, and most recently Dover's
1968 edition, is a unique achievement in Indian literature.

II *Mythological Background of Songs*

The significance of the translated songs is immeasurably en-
hanced by the collector's inclusion of the myths or legends that

gave rise to them. For example, Curtis wrote of the Navajo "Mountain Songs" that they

describe a journey to a holy place beyond the sacred mountains where are everlasting life and blessedness. The Divine Ones who live in and beyond the mountains made the songs, and so they tell of the journey as of a homecoming.

When these songs are sung over a man, the spirit of the man makes the journey that the song describes. Upon the rainbow he moves from mountain to mountain, for it is thus that the gods travel, standing upon the rainbow. . . .

The mountain protects man like a god. When a man sings of the mountain, then, through the singing, his spirit goes to the holy place beyond the mountain, and he himself becomes like the mountain, pure and holy, living eternally, forever blessed.[3]

Thus, these songs demonstrate the dominant trait of Indian poetry, its spiritual or exalted quality. Nowhere does Curtis better portray the majesty of this feeling than in the "Mountain Songs" of the Navajo:

> Swift and far I journey,
> Swift upon the rainbow.
> Swift and far I journey,
> Lo, yonder, the Holy Place!
>   Yea, swift and far I journey.
> To Sisnajinni, and beyond it,
>   Yea, swift and far I journey;
> The Chief of Mountains, and beyond it,
>   Yea, swift and far I journey;
> To Life Unending, and beyond it,
>   Yea, swift and far I journey;
> To Joy Unchanging, and beyond it,
>   Yea, swift and far I journey.[4]

These holy mountain songs were sung as part of the healing ceremonies for persons who were ill. The quotation is the first of six songs, each of which was sung four times with another mountain's name substituted in each sixth line. They were sung not too slowly but quietly.

In Navajo mythology, "Sisnajinni" is a sacred mountain placed "to the East" by First-Man and First-Woman. They decorated it with white shell and secured it to the earth by a lightning bolt. First-Man and First-Woman covered it with a sheet of daylight and placed Dawn Youth and Dawn Maiden to reside in it. First-Man and First-Woman placed other holy mountains to the south, west, and north; they adorned them, respectively, with turquoise, haliotis shell, cannel coal; and they fastened them to the earth with a stone knife, a sunbeam, and a rainbow. Then First-Man and First-Woman covered the south mountain with blue sky and placed Turquoise Youth and Turquoise Maid to live in it. They covered the west mountain with a yellow cloud and placed Twilight Youth and Haliotis Maiden as dwellers therein. After covering the north mountain with darkness, they put Youth of Cannel Coal and Darkness Maid as residents. The center mountain they decorated with striped agate, and here the first Navajos were created. These gems (coal included), which were used as sacred offerings to the holy ones, accorded with Navajo color symbolism—white for the east; turquoise (blue) for the south; yellow for the west; black for the north. To a Navajo, "Chief of Mountains" means something higher and holier than the term "chief" implies, "because the Navajo sings to the mountain as to a god."[5]

The Navajo are the largest surviving Indian tribe in the United States today. They are semi-nomadic, pastoral people who cultivate corn patches but who also roam the desert canyons and the red rock mesas seeking pasturage and water holes for their flocks of sheep and goats. Their reservation spreads over the Four Corners country—Monument Valley in southeastern Utah; northeastern Arizona; northwestern New Mexico; and southwestern Colorado.

As has already been noted, Navajo poetry is characterized by elaborate, intense ritualism, and it abounds in long chants. A great variety in theme and imagery also marks their songs and chants. Although such variety is found in Indian verse in general, it is particularly prevalent in the songs of the Navajo, the Zuñi, and the Pawnee "Hako." Because of numerous preludes and refrains to the verses, music plays an important role in Navajo rites. Curtis described the chanting as having a quiet, monotonous quality and as being performed with dedicated concentration by the singers to prevent error in word or in song sequence. Their dramatic "Mountain Chant" (called "Mountain Songs" by Curtis) is considered outstanding for its beautiful poetic imagery, and it is rated one of the finest examples of Indian verse translated into English.

III Subjective Element in Poetry

The Indian poet rarely gives voice to introspective song. But the "Wind-Songs," translated by Curtis from the Kiowa, are good examples of subjective Indian verse. These songs also demonstrate the Native American belief in the power of thought directed by one person or group of persons towards another. The helpful power of the thought is not nullified by the absence of the person to whom the thought is directed.[6] These very old songs express a longing for loved ones absent on the warpath. They are called "Wind-Songs" because they are "songs of loneliness and longing like the open prairie where there is only the sweep of the wind."[7]

> Idlers and cowards are here at home now,
>
> Whenever they wish, they see their beloved ones.
>
> Oh, idlers and cowards are here at home now,
>
> But the youth I love is gone to war, far hence.
>
> Weary, lonely, for me he longs.[8]

II

> I have but one love,
> I have but one love,
> I have but one love,
> And he is far away,
>   On the war-path, e-ye, e-ye!
>   Lonely are the days and weary.[9]

The Kiowa sought spiritual guidance in the cult of the Mescal religion. Curtis noted that this very ancient faith had spread from the Kiowa to other Plains tribes (Comanche, Arapahoe, Cheyenne, even to the Northern Winnebago in Nebraska). The peyote, a round, mescal-button, symbolized the sun, the source of life. The ceremony began in a teepee at night and lasted until dawn. During the religious curative rites, which were accompanied by singing, shaking of rattles, and the beating of a drum, the participants ate at least four peyote cactus buds to induce a vision. Since the mescal faith enjoined cleanliness, the worshipers went to bathe in a river upon the ceremony's conclusion. The songs—each was sung four times—contained no words; the syllables were esoteric in meaning, and the songs were an invocation for the revelation of universal truths. The peyote religion seems equivalent to the vision-seeking quest for the spirit-helper of other Plains tribes. Young men fasted and prayed for four days and nights in an isolated spot, and hoped the spirit-guide would give them, through a vision, a magic formula, a song, or instructions to help them in daily life. Additionally, modern cult followers believed that mescal cured them of tuberculosis and drunkenness—two of their inheritances from the white race. At least one medical authority claimed mescal was not only an efficacious cardiac stimulant but also a respiratory medicine useful in treating asthma.[10]

IV *Sensuous Beauty in Native American Songs*

Indian verse is generally rich in the sensuous beauty, the lights and shadows, and the colors and sounds of the world of nature. The Hopi "Katzina Songs"[11] furnish especially good illustrations of these qualities. The "Katzinas," go-between deities who carry the prayers of the Hopi to the gods, formerly lived upon the earth, danced in the villages, and brought rain. Now, since these deities no longer come to earth, the Hopi impersonate them both in dress and by wearing wooden, symbolically painted masks as they dance and sing like the Katzinas of old in order to bring the rains. These songs express a lyrical joy in the poetry of motion, and Curtis transcribes their rhythm particulary well in her translations, especially in the "Anga Katzina Song":[12]

> Rain all over the cornfields,
> Pretty butterfly-maidens
> Chasing one another when the rain is done,

Hither, thither, so.
How they frolic 'mid the corn,

Laughing, laughing, thus:

A-ha, ha-ha,
O-ah, e-lo!

How they frolic 'mid the corn,

Singing, singing, thus:

O-o, o-ho,
O-he, e-lo!

This song was composed by Lahpu, a member of Oraibi's oldest clan, who had returned to his native village after a long absence. He was so overjoyed at beholding Hopi girls chasing each other, laughing, and singing among the green corn plants, that he composed his first song about the girls. The maids were called "butterfly-girls" by the young men because their hair style made them appear like the insects' wings. The songs were sung moderately fast and accompanied by gourd rattles.

In another poem, the "He-Hea Katzina Song,"[13] the young corn plants are likened to maidens who are blossoming into womanhood:

Corn-blossom maidens
Here in the fields,
Patches of beans in flower,
Fields all abloom,
Water shining after rain,
Blue clouds looming above.

Now behold!
Through bright clusters of flowers
Yellow butterflies
Are chasing at play,
And through the blossoming beans
Blue butterflies
Are chasing at play.

V   Hopi Traditions and Culture

Unlike their once-warlike Navajo neighbors, whose reservation surrounds that of the Hopi in northeastern Arizona, these Indians were peaceful village dwellers who built their adobe and stone houses atop sheer cliffs. Old Oraibi, their modern town, which has been lived in over 800 years, is the oldest continuously occupied settlement in the United States. Their eleven communities on three mesas were so located for safety from marauders. Precipitous trails led down to the corn and bean fields in the desert plain where the flocks were driven daily to forage for food.

Although the Hopi are one of the oldest tribal groups to inhabit the southwest, their culture, Curtis learned when she visited their reservation, has been least affected by European impact. Their traditions are rich in myths and legends. Myths revolve around the questions: "Who are we? Where did we come from? Why are we in this world? Where are we going?"[14] Many myths repeat the theme of how certain ancient villages were destroyed "in the struggle between good and evil."[15]

Besides the "Four Worlds" appearing in their myth of emergence, or story of creation, the Hopi likewise celebrated four principal rituals—the Two Horn, the One Horn, the Flute, and the Wuwuchim—that were derivative from the Katzina (or Kachina) cult. Since the songs that accompany the rites are similar in purpose and in words to "clouds" for the "rain hither come"—only the Flute, the Wuwuchim, and the Snake ceremonials, as typical ones, will be discussed. The Flute ceremony was a prayer for the replenishment of water in the springs; it was performed in alternate years with the Snake dance. When the priests conducted sacred rites around a spring on the ritual's ninth day, some sang the appropriate songs; others played the same melody on flutes. Each Hopi village had two flute societies, the Blue and the Gray (the significance of which Curtis did not explain) whose mutual purpose was to summon thundershowers.[16]

A thanksgiving ceremony, called Wuwuchim-yungya, was performed following the corn harvest. The men, singing and dancing throughout the night, visited one *kiva* (underground ceremonial pit) after another. Such *kivas,* Curtis explained, were used by men as places to meet in council, to spin and to weave, to learn new songs, and to practice dances. Most importantly, *kivas* were used as sacred chambers in which altars were placed and secret ceremonial rites held. The men gave thanks for the harvest that came from Stepmother Corn, and they also invoked the gods through song-prayers to insure bountiful crops for the ensuing year. Song accompanied the ceremonial planting of a perfect corn-ear in the hope of begetting equally perfect corn the next season. The Hopi men (*kivas* tabu to women) also addressed prayers to Muyingwa, god of germination and growth, who lived beneath the *kivas*.[17]

The Snake dance is probably the Hopi's most spectacular rain-making ceremony. Even today the dancers drape live rattlers across their shoulders while holding both ends of the vipers in their hands. Sometimes they even grasp the serpent's body between their teeth. Although the snakes are not defanged, a dancer is seldom struck because "huggers" stroke the reptiles with feather-tipped sticks to distract their attention. Rattlesnakes are a sacred symbol, "conceived of as messengers entrusted with prayers," according to a recent investigator.[18] Both the Snake and the Corn dance ceremonials are accompanied by singing, and are performed as seasonal rituals.

Hopi as individuals are given to spontaneous songs on all occasions, Curtis commented, and lullabies are among their most ancient ones. Music springs from their environment, she observed, but to commit it to paper was for the recorder as impossible a task "as to put on canvas the shimmer and glare of the desert."

VI   *Indian Verse Rich in Imagery*

The Indian poet's variety of imagery is as variegated and multifarious as the outdoors. This Pima "Wind-Song,"[19] a Medicine Song, is a fine example of sense imagery that even in translation retains its onomatopoetic effect of movement, and, of course, it is sung slowly:

> Far on the desert ridges
>   Stands the cactus;
> Lo, the blossoms swaying
> To and fro, the blossoms swaying,
>   swaying.

Numerous other illustrations from Curtis' translations of other tribes' verse might be cited, as for instance, the imagery of color in the "Katzina Songs" already quoted, or in the Navajo "War-Song" of the Flint Youth and in this excerpt from the Navajo "The Song of the Earth":[20]

> And the white corn,
> And the yellow corn.

VII *The Ancient Pima*

Southern Arizona is the ancestral homeland of the Pima, who were skillful basket makers and who were, like the Hopi, a peaceable people. Living in the semi-arid river valleys, they irrigated their crops through a system of canals, and they were growing and weaving cotton before the Spaniards arrived. Archaeologists believe them to be descendants of the ancient Anasazi, who inhabited the area of the Salt and Gila River valleys about 9,000 years ago. Curtis found that the Pima had lost most of their old identity, their dances, and their ceremonials. But their surviving songs and music, she noted, had a plaintive quality, their myths were beautiful, and nearly all their dance songs were named for birds. An aged Pima medicine man and chief told Curtis that Pimans dreamed their songs in solitude. *The Indians' Book* contains only three examples of Pima poetry.

Another researcher and translator, Frank Russell, collected Pima song-myths of tribal origin; game, hunting, and festal songs; medicine and healing songs for every kind of ailment; rain and war songs; and songs for the puberty ceremony. Russell's translations of these songs were published in 1908 under the title of "The Pima Indians" in the Bureau of American Ethnology's *Twenty-Sixth Annual Report*. Two of the transcriptions are worth quoting, not only for their aesthetic quality but because the first one, Russell's "Wind Song,"[21] a Medicine Song, reveals the Indian's keen description of nature in a vein similar to Curtis's "Wind-Song." In Russell's case, the poem's sound imagery suggests a thunderous wind's movement as it sweeps over the desert with gale force:

> Wind now commences to sing;
> > Wind now commences to sing.
> The land stretches before me,
> > Before me stretches away.

> Wind's house now is thundering;
>> Wind's house now is thundering.
> I go roaring o'er the land,
>> The land covered with thunder.
>
> Over the windy mountains;
>> Over the windy mountains,
> Came the myriad-legged wind;
>> The wind came running hither.
>
> The Black Snake Wind came to me;
>> The Black Snake Wind came to me,
> Came and wrapped itself about,
>> Came here running with its song.

Curtis observed that Pima dance songs were usually named for birds. Russell's "Swallow Song,"[22] which illustrates this Pima preference, was sung during a social dance by men and women together. Russell's translation is an example of an infrequent lyric type of social dance song, and the quotations in these pages from his and Curtis's collections demonstrate that Pima songs are full of movement and sound, although sound imagery is rare in Indian verse. The swallow sings for rain in this Russell rendition:

> Now the Swallow begins his singing;
>> Now the Swallow begins his singing.
> And the women who are with me,
>> The poor women commence to sing.
>
> The Swallows met in the standing cliffs;
>> The Swallows met in the standing cliffs.
> And the rainbows arched above me,
>> There the blue rainbow arches met.

This is a "circling song" which was "accompanied by dancing and the beating of baskets. The dancers moved in a circle made up of men and women alternately"; for, as one male dancer confided, " 'it looks bad for two men to be together.' "[23]

VIII *Repetition in Native American Poesy*

Although Curtis's translations from the Pima were only token ones, her collection contains many poems from other tribes that exhibit the diversity of aesthetic qualities of Native American poetic style. For instance, another universal element found in Indian verse, it will be recalled, is repetition. In her transcription of a traditional Zuñi "Corn-Grinding Song,"[24] Curtis brought out the artistic value of the monotonous repetition of phrases. The movements of the women as they bend over their metates while grinding the corn accompany the rhythm of this song, which is sung quietly though not too slowly. The rainbow symbolizes the Rainbow Youth who is "brightly decked and painted"; the swallow, the Zuñis believe, sings for rain.

> Yonder, yonder see the fair rainbow,
> See the rainbow brightly decked and painted!
> Now the swallow bringeth glad news to your corn,
> Singing, "Hitherward, hitherward, hitherward, rain,
>   "Hither come!"
> Singing, "Hitherward, hitherward, hitherward, white
>   cloud, "Hither come!"
> Now hear the corn-plants murmur,
> "We are growing everywhere!"
> IIi, yai! The world, how fair!

Using metates, the women made a social affair of the endless corn-grinding chores; they lightened their work by bursting into song. Often the men stood by playing an accompaniment on the flute.

IX *Personification in Indian Poetry*

Another typical trait of Indian verse is personification.[25] Clouds, sun, moon, stars, rainbows, plants, and animals are given the power to utter human speech and express human feelings. For example, the corn ear expresses a hope for rain in another Zuñi "Corn-Grinding Song."[26] This one is sung by the young men quietly but not too slowly while the young women, kneeling at the stone metates, grind the corn into meal:

> Lovely! See the cloud, the cloud appear!
> Lovely, See the rain, the rain draw near!
>   Who spoke?
> 'Twas the little corn-ear

> High on the tip of the stalk
> Saying while it looked at me
> Talking aloft there—
> "Ah, perchance the floods
> Hither moving—
> Ah, may the floods come this way!"

This song is also both old and traditional that, fortunately, Curtis preserved and recorded. Corn is the main staple of the Pueblo peoples. After grinding the corn with a stone in the trough of a flat rock slab, the maidens danced to the accompaniment of the flute and the drum played by the youths.

X Zuñi Rituals and Song-Prayers

Besides their lyric poems, Zuñi culture is also noted for ancient ceremonial rites accompanied by song-prayers. As Curtis collected only Zuñi corn-grinding lyrics, a description of their ritual formulas and poetic traits will supplement her work. Pedro de Castañeda, the Spanish chronicler of Coronado's 1540 expedition, recorded that tribal priests, who were elder brothers called "pekwin," recited prayers at dawn from the highest roof of the village before the assembled people. The form of Zuñi prayers has probably changed little since Coronado's conquest, according to ethnologist Ruth Bunzel's extensive study. She stated:

Prayer in Zuñi is not a spontaneous outpouring of the heart. It is rather the repetition of a fixed formula. Only in such prayers as those accompanying individual offerings of corn meal and food is a certain amount of individual variation possible, and even here variation is restricted to the matter of abridgment or inclusiveness. The general form of the prayer, the phraseology and the nature of the request, conform strictly to types for other prayers.[27]

In the *kivas*, each father taught his son the proper prayers since there were many to suit various needs. Rare, secret prayers, or ones believed to possess great magical power, had a high monetary value and could be sold by the possessor. An example of a Zuñi song-prayer is this invocation to the sun at dawn:

> Now this day,
> My sun father,

Now that you have come out standing to your sacred place,
That from which we draw the water of life,
Prayer meal,
Here I give to you.
Your long life,
Your old age,
Your waters,
Your seeds,
Your riches,
Your power,
Your strong spirit,
All these to me may you grant.[28]

The ritual formulas practiced by the Zuñi are found in North American tribes generally, and many ritual acts were accompanied by songs. There were, Bunzel observed, "special song sequences for setting up and taking down altars, for mixing medicine water or soapsuds, for bathing the head at initiations, to accompany various acts of curing," and for many other Zuñi village activities. Like prayers, ritual acts "must be learned ritualistically.... Certain women also have grinding songs in addition to the well-known songs of the men."[29]

Annually, around Thanksgiving time, the Zuñi celebrate with song-prayer and dancing the winter solstice Shalako festival, which, according to Bernice Johnston of the Arizona State Museum in Tucson, is "one of the most serious, impressive, important ceremonies held by any Southwest Indian tribe."[30] This masked ritual dance is performed by the Shalako *kachinas* (intermediary deities between the Zuñi people and the gods) who come not only to pray for rain, bountiful crops, health, and long life, but also to bless new homes for all peoples everywhere. Six Shalako dancers "represent birds from the four [cardinal] directions, the zenith and nadir," and they are the larger bird species as symbolic of the "giant couriers of the rainmakers."[31] Ceremonies, which begin late in the day and continue intermittently throughout the night, concluding in the morning, are accompanied by songs and litanies.

Johnston offers no examples of Shalako song-prayers, but Bunzel, who gives the festival name as Ca'lako, translated numerous examples of lengthy ritual songs in the *Forty-Seventh*

Annual Report of the Bureau of American Ethnology (1930). The songs are sung by the dancers over a period of days during both winter and spring solstices. For example, the following is a partial quotation of the "Prayer of the Impersonators of the Masked Gods with Monthly Offering of Prayer Sticks" from the Ca'lako winter ceremonial chant. This one phase of the ceremony lasted for two weeks.

> This is all.
> Thus with plain words we have passed you on your roads.
> Now we fulfill the thoughts of our fathers.
> Always with one thought
> We shall live together.
>
> This is all.
> Thus with plain words we have passed you on your roads.
> For whatever our fathers desired
> When at the New Year
> They sent forth their sacred words,
> We have now fulfilled their thoughts.
> To this end: My fathers,
> My mothers,
> My children,
> Always with one thought
> May we live together.
> With your waters,
> Your seeds,
> Your riches,
> Your power,
> Your strong spirit,
> All your good fortune,
> With all this may you bless us.[32]

The chief features of Zuñi poetic ritual style, Bunzel found, are fixed metaphors as in the phrases the sun always "comes out standing to this sacred place" (exemplified in the quoted invocation to the sun at dawn), and corn plants "stretch out their hands to all directions calling for rain." Other stylistic devices include a refrain repeated after every line to achieve a pattern, and the fact that all ritualistic verse is expressed in an irregular length of line (as in the two quoted passages in this section).

XI *Varied Uses of Repetition*

Besides the Zuñi "Corn-Grinding Songs," we also find repetition put to other artistic uses in Curtis's transcriptions from the Navajo. Repetition in the "Song of the Horse" (quoted previously) is saved from monotony through the use of striking imagery; but in the "Mountain Songs" (excerpt quoted previously), repetition carries the action forward. This use of a repeated refrain is also found in the "Hunting-Song,"[33] which is sung with spirit:

> Comes the deer to my singing,
> Comes the deer to my song,
> Comes the deer to my singing.
>
> He, the blackbird, he am I,
> Bird beloved of the wild deer.
> > Comes the deer to my singing.
>
> From the Mountain Black,
> From the summit,
> Down the trail, coming, coming now,
> > Comes the deer to my singing.
>
> Through the blossoms,
> Through the flowers, coming, coming now,
> > Comes the deer to my singing.

This ancient invocation for good hunting, the legend states, is sung by the Navajo hunter after praying to Hastyeyalti, the god of sunrise and of game. It was believed that if the hunter remained still and chanted the song (of which the above is an extract) without error, the deer, charmed by the singing, would approach close enough to receive a fatal arrow from the hunter's bow. The Navajo believe the god Hastyeyalti made this and other ancient hunting songs and gave them to their ancestors in the old days before their people became shepherds, for their flocks of sheep and goats were only acquired after the Spanish conquest.

In the Pima "Song of the World,"[34] repetition is used as a device for emphasis. This poem is a good sample of the interlacing verse pattern that is achieved by alternation of the lines.

The song refers to the myth that recounts the creation of the world by a creator who rolled a ball of greasewood gum under his feet in the pristine darkness. As he stood upon the ball and rolled it under his foot, he sang:

> I make the world, and lo!
> The world is finished.
> Thus I make the world, and lo!
> The world is finished.
> > Let it go, let it go,
> > Let it go, start it forth!

As he slowly sang, the ball grew larger until it became the world by the end of the chant, and the last two lines were sung in quick tempo. The myth also related how the world maker made stars and the moon of rock—knowledge which modern astronauts have discovered.

Another archaic Pima "creation song" that employed the same characteristic traits of Indian verse—repetition for emphasis, interlacing design by alternation of the lines, and incremental repetition with the intensity increasing at the close of the poem —contrasts in interesting fashion with the foregoing lyric because these stylistic devices appear in each song. The following translation is by Frank Russell:

The Creation of the Earth[35]

> Earth Magician shapes this world.
> > Behold what he can do!
> Round and smooth he molds it.
> > Behold what he can do!
> Earth Magician makes the mountains.
> > Heed what he has to say!
> He it is that makes the mesas.
> > Heed what he has to say.
> Earth Magician shapes this world;
> > Earth Magician makes its Mountains;
> Makes all larger, larger, larger.
> > Into the earth the Magician glances;
> Into its mountains he may see.

Another use of repetition in Curtis's translation of the "Song of the Hogans"[36] serves as a refrain for a series of beautiful pictures. "Hogan" is a Navajo word for a dwelling, used here to symbolize the sacred abodes of the Sun-God—Hastyeyalti in the east, and Hastyhogan, God of Sunset, in the west. The song is one of the oldest of the Hozhonji (holy) songs (as distinguished from medicine songs) and it is sung very quietly and evenly. The Navajo believe these chants of peace and of blessing were given to them by the gods to protect their people against all evil, and have been compared to the Psalms of David:

> Lo, yonder the hogan,
>> The hogan blessed!
>
> There beneath the sunrise
>> Standeth the hogan,
>> The hogan blessed.
>
> Of Hastyeyalti-ye
>> The hogan,
>> The hogan blessed.
>
> Built of dawn's first light
>> Standeth his hogan,
>> The hogan blessed.
>
> Built of fair white corn
>> Standeth his hogan,
>> The hogan blessed.
>
> Built of broidered ropes and hides
>> Standeth his hogan,
>> The hogan blessed.
>
> Built of mixed All-Waters pure
>> Standeth his hogan,
>> The hogan blessed.
>
> Built of holy pollen
>> Standeth his hogan,
>> The hogan blessed.
>
> Evermore enduring,
> Happy evermore,
>> His hogan,
>> The hogan blessed.

The number of repetitions used has a distinct significance to the Native American mind, although it may seem monotonous or accidental to other readers. The Indian's world, for instance, is divided into fours: "four seasons, four divisions of a day or a life, and, above all, four World Corners—the cardinal or semi-cardinal directions."[37]

XII   The Indians' Book *as a Significant Achievement*

The high literary standard of Curtis's translations in *The Indians' Book* may be used as a measure for other translated Indian poetry and for the studies of that poetry's subject matter and form. No other writer's work in this field transcribes more faithfully the Indian's song literature. As an outstanding translator, she is deeply deserving of praise for her interpretations of the poems in the context of their legendary and traditional backgrounds. For this reason, the songs acquire a richness and a significant connotation which they otherwise would not have had for the non-Indian reader. In all of her output, she sedulously presented the Indian's simple, straightforward, but often naive mode of expression, using rhythm-patterns that are peculiar to his sense of harmony, including repetition, alternating and parallel rhythm, and the interlacing type of design by alternation of the lines. Besides, the poetry is expressed in the Imagist's free-verse form, which, in Austin's opinion, originated with the North American Indians.

We are indeed fortunate that the materials were gathered at the turn of the century, for the old people even then, as Curtis remarked, "walked in the sunset hour of their native life and . . . the night was soon to come."[38] It would be impossible to compile such a book today with its wealth of content. This unusual volume, reviewed in Europe as well as in America, won recognition "not only for the amazing accuracy of the musical transcriptions, but for the revelation of the Indian's artistic genius and for the light which it shed on the inner thought and aspirations of primitive man."[39]

CHAPTER 6

Alice Corbin Henderson (1881–1949)

A comparatively recent writer who has dealt with Indian subjects and rhythms, and whose work is of a uniformly high quality, is Alice Corbin Henderson. The young Alice Corbin found her forte in poetry, and her first volume of verse, *Linnet Songs* (1898), was published when she was seventeen. A year later, she was graduated from Chicago's Hyde Park High School and entered the University of Chicago in the fall, attending until 1902. Then, having inherited a predisposition to tuberculosis (which had caused her mother's death when Alice was three), she was sent to New Orleans to improve her health by her father. Alice continued her education there at Sophie Newcomb College and became a book reviewer for the *Times-Picayune*. When she returned to Chicago the fall of 1903, she wrote reviews for the *Tribune* and *Evening Post*.

While attending Chicago's Academy of Fine Arts, Alice Corbin met Instructor William Penhallow Henderson, an artist and architect, whom she married on October 14, 1905. Their daughter, Alice Oliver, was born in Chicago on January 27, 1907. The family toured Europe in 1910 and returned to Chicago in September, 1911. Between 1912 and 1916, Henderson became a cosponsor and coeditor of *Poetry Magazine* with Harriet Monroe, and she continued as associate editor from 1916 to 1922. She and Monroe compiled *The New Poetry*, an anthology published in New York in 1917, which they revised in 1923 and of which they prepared in 1932 a new edition.

When Henderson moved with her family from Chicago to the literary and art colony in Santa Fé, New Mexico, in March, 1916, she came into direct contact with Indian life and literature. Her health problems had forced the permanent move to Santa Fé, and

Henderson had to spend a year in a sanitarium before recovering her physical vigor. Henderson soon became publicity chairman for the Woman's Auxiliary of the State Board of Defense in Santa Fé upon America's entrance into World War I in 1917. By 1925, a group of Santa Fé poets met weekly at the Henderson home to read their poems, and they later met at various homes to raise money for the Southwest Indian Association. Within two years, she helped other members of the literati in organizing the Spanish Colonial Arts Society and Indian Arts Fund. When in 1933 the literary colony's writers decided to establish the regional publishing house Writer's Editions, Alice assisted them, and she contributed a general collection of verse, *The Sun Turns West.* She also served as editor-in-chief for New Mexico's project of the American Guide Series in 1936, for which she wrote the chapter "Literature," and continued her editing duties until July, 1937. Meanwhile, she had become a librarian and curator for the Museum of Navaho Ceremonial Art in Santa Fé. The building had been designed by her husband.

Alice devoted her creative energies in 1939 to giving a lecture course at Santa Fé's Arsuna School and Art Gallery. The next year she assisted in planning a historical pageant, combined with a series of statewide rodeos, fiestas, and conferences, to celebrate New Mexico's Coronado Cuarto-Centennial, 1540–1940. After the death of her husband on October 15, 1943, at Tesuque Pueblo, Alice Henderson became active in the Association on American-Indian Affairs, the Indian Arts Fund, the Laboratory of Anthropology, and the Museum of Navaho Ceremonial Art. Although she wrote no more poetry, she made a disc recording in 1947 of six of her favorite poems.

These numerous civic, editorial, and art activities left Henderson little time or energy for her creative expression. She wrote only one volume of native and New Mexico verse, *Red Earth* (1920), which comprised in its fifty-four pages nine of her experimental Indian songs. Six of them appeared in *The Path on the Rainbow.* An anthology of New Mexico poetry, *The Turquoise Trail,* published in Boston and New York in 1928, includes some Indian chants by the well-known ethnologist-translator Herbert Joseph Spinden and by interpreters Mary Austin and Eda Lou Walton.

I *Imagist Influence on "Indian Keynote"*

Henderson as an editor was enthusiastic about both the current interest in imagism and about Native American song literature as a new medium for poetic art. As a result, Henderson's early work shows a strong imagist tendency, and she favors the free verse form. This influence is noticeable in her Indian poetry, which is cast in the repetitive patterns typical of the Indian's poetic expression. Her output may be classed as interpretative because she takes the "Indian keynote," never borrows more than a phrase or a single image, and expands it "very slightly."[1] Her poem "Listening"[2] has sound imagery for its keynote, and it is a rare example of the Indian's interpretation of a sound:

> The noise of passing feet
> On the prairie—
> Is it men or gods
> Who come out of the silence?

II *Compared with Translations*

How effectively Henderson captured the essence of Indian poetic thought in "Listening" may be seen in Frances Densmore's translation of the original, "They are Playing a Game":[3]

> The noise of passing feet
> on the prairie
> They are playing a game as they come
> Those men.

The occasion for the song, Densmore explained, happened during the return home of a Chippewa war party when one warrior sank exhausted to the ground. His companions remained nearby to protect him from any lurking enemies. Although it seemed impossible for him to go on, "he used his medicine, and after a time sprang to his feet, singing this song, which he composed at the time. The war-party resumed its journey, and he accompanied them, still singing his new song."[4] The words "playing a game" are an allusion to the Chippewa's favorite game of lacrosse.

The poem, "Listening," and the six following, Henderson staetd, were all "based on the literal translations [from the Chippewa] made by Miss Frances Densmore."[5] Thus, Henderson's compositions actually are, like Austin's, poetic re-expressions from original translations, of which her "Buffalo Dance" is another typical sample. In the original chant, the Chippewa imitated the actions of the bison while performing a war dance. As translated by Densmore in *Bulletin 53* of the Bureau of American Ethnology, this chant appeared as the "Song of the Buffalo":[6]

> Strike ye
>   Our land
>   With curved horns.

Henderson expanded it "very slightly," and the "Indian keynote" emerged from her gifted pen as "Buffalo Dance":[7]

> Strike ye our land
> With curved horns!
> Now with cries
> Bending our bodies,
> Breathe fire upon us;
> Now with feet
> Trampling the earth,
> Let your hoofs
> Thunder over us!
> Strike ye our land
> With curved horns!

The reinterpretation retains the irregularity of rhythm and straightforward expression so characteristic of Indian verse. However, the phrasing savors of Anglo-Saxon as well as Indian terseness. But the chant expresses a feeling of motion, and it produces the "effect of rugged strength" that was intended, according to Densmore, by the native chanters.

III   *Iterative Repetition for Artistic Effect*

In the next poem—Densmore's "On the Bank of a Stream," from which Henderson evidently borrowed the "keynote" for her interpretative version, "Where the Fight Was"—Henderson employs the iterative type of repetition. The original poem "On the Bank of a Stream"[8] is based on a Chippewa war dance song that Densmore collected. This song is presumed to have been composed in honor of the warriors in a celebrated battle on a river bank between the Chippewa and the Sioux, their mortal enemies. Densmore's literal rendition reads:

> Across the river
> They speak of me as being.

In Henderson's version, "Where the Fight Was,"[9] the song has been transformed by her imagination to give it an emotional appeal, and it is couched in less obscure phrasing:

> In the place where the fight was
> Across the river,
> In the place where the fight was
> Across the river:
> A heavy load for a woman
> To lift in her blanket,
> A heavy load for a woman
> To carry on her shoulder.
> In the place where the fight was
> Across the river,
> In the place where the fight was
> Across the river:
> The women go wailing
> To gather the wounded
> The women go wailing
> To pick up the dead.

Another comparison is Henderson's interpretation of "The Wind" and the cryptic meaning of Densmore's original "Carried Around the Sky." The translation is a Dream Song chanted by a medicine man in connection with a Chippewa healing ceremony:

> As the wind is carrying me
> Around the sky.[10]

Henderson's rendition introduces a slight variance in thought expressed through repetition for emphasis, and it suggests man's spirit being airborne:

The Wind[11]

The wind is carrying me round the sky;
The wind is carrying me round the sky.
My body is here in the valley—
The wind is carrying me round the sky.

Much of the value of this last poem is lost because Henderson did not explain the origin, traditions, or customs that gave rise to it. Densmore tells how, before treating the sick, the Chippewa medicine man fasted in a retreat to which he believed the *manidó* (spirit) "came to give him the power to do his work." Ill persons were treated by singing over the patient; by shaking a rattle; by passing hands over the sick one's prone body; and, in the song quoted, by "apparently swallowing one or more bones, which are afterward removed from his [doctor's] mouth."[12] "Carried Around the Sky," is then sung after the "doctor" has "swallowed the bones and during the treatment of the sick person."[13] The medicine men usually got their songs through dreams or visions. Such songs could not be either bought or sold, and their meanings were often deliberately cryptic.

Though Henderson's song "Fear"[14] is typical of Indian poetry in its abrupt beginning, its brevity, its emotional high crest, and its interlacing repetition through alternation of the lines, it too needs to be interpreted for the non-Indian reader:

The odor of death
In the front of my body,
The odor of death
Before me—

Is there any one
Who would weep for me?
My wife
Would weep for me.

According to Densmore, who has again supplied the needed clues to the poem, it is the "Death-Song of Namebines,"[15] a Chippewa warrior chief, who composed it as he lay dying in a clump of bushes after a victory over the Sioux. "Looking into the faces of his comrades he said, 'When you reach home sing this for the women to dance by and tell them how I died.' "[16] In the ethnologist's literal rendering, this song came forth as:

> The odor of death,
>   I discern the odor of death
>   In the front of my body.

IV Pseudo-Anglo-Saxon Influence

The last two poems in this group of Henderson's Chippewa interpretations, "Courtship" and "Parting," have a polished turn of phrase and a precision of rhythm that apparently show the influence of Anglo-Saxon form and, therefore, a loss in distinctively Indian quality. This loss is especially evident in the lines of "Courtship,"[17] which are almost like a Mother Goose rhyme:

> When I go I will give you surely
> What you will wear if you go with me;
> A blanket of red and a bright girdle,
> Two new moccasins and a silver necklace.
> When I go I will give you surely
> What you will wear if you go with me!

It is surprising to discover that the repetitious lines are quoted verbatim by Henderson from Densmore's free translation, called "Go with Me":[18]

> When I go
> I will give you surely
> What you will wear
> If you go with me.

This courting song contains when sung, Densmore explains, "an indefinable element of pleading."[19]

The next Chippewa song, "Do Not Weep,"[20] may concern either the departure of a lover, Densmore states, or loss and longing:

> Do not weep
> Now I go
> Do not weep.

Henderson elected in her interpretation, "Parting,"[21] to expand the thought in both significance and emotional appeal, and to make the song suggestive of the Indian's belief in immortality:

> Now I go, do not weep, woman—
> Woman, do not weep;
> Though I go from you to die,
> We shall both lie down
> At the foot of the hill, and sleep.
>
> Now I go, do not weep, woman—
> Woman, do not weep;
> Earth is our mother and our tent the sky.
> Though I go from you to die,
> We shall both lie down
> At the foot of the hill, and sleep.

V   A *Pueblo Interpretation*

Henderson follows the Indian motif strictly in the "Corn-Grinding Song."[22] It was given to her by Canuto Suaza, a Tesuque Indian, who translated it in both Spanish and English from the Tewa language. Her "rendering is as direct as possible."[23] Its succesful capture of the full flavor of Indian verse indicates her ability to have produced more such works:

> This way from the north
> Comes the cloud,
> Very blue,
> And inside the cloud is the blue corn.
>
> > How beautiful the cloud
> > Bringing corn of blue color!
>
> This way from the west
> Comes the cloud,
> Very yellow,
> And inside the cloud is the yellow corn.
>
> > How beautiful the cloud
> > Bringing corn of yellow color!
>
> This way from the south
> Comes the cloud,
> Very red,
> And inside the cloud is the red corn.

> How beautiful the cloud
> Bringing corn of red color!

The next stanza repeats the first,, except the direction "east" is used in the first line, and "white" is substituted in the third and fourth lines, and in the last line of the refrain. The poem concludes:

> How beautiful the clouds
> From the north and the west
> From the south and the east
> Bringing corn of all colors!

Another version of the "Corn Grinding Song of Tesuque," translated by Spinden, is an interesting contrast to Henderson's poem. Only the opening stanza is quoted, for the next three stanzas vary only in the directions and colors used:

> There towards the north,
> There the fog is lying,
> There the fog is lying.
> In the middle stands Blue Corn
> Happily, prettily, she is singing
> Ha-we-ra-na na-a-se.[24]

Spinden notes that the Corn Maiden in each stanza is named in accordance with the accepted color symbolism.[25] These two versions vividly portray the differences between the two styles. Henderson depended on a Tewa Indian for her translation, which she, as a poet, transformed through her creative imagination into an artistically balanced lyric. Spinden, an ethnologist-translator, recorded a literal transcription of the same song, much as it would appear to the Indian's mind.

Tesuque village is the southernmost of six Tewa or Tehua Indian pueblos along the Rio Grande River Valley about eight miles north of Santa Fé, New Mexico. The Tewa, who were practicing agriculture when discovered by the Spaniards, also occupy the pueblos of San Ildefonso, San Juan, Santa Clara, Nambe, and Hano. Each village is divided by birthright groups into sections of winter and summer people, and each has its ruling *cacique* (chief).[26] Herbert Joseph Spinden is the outstanding translator of Tewa poetry.

The fact that seasonal rains were so important to the Tewa food supply is reflected in the songs of the many rain rituals. These songs often express striking imagery, such as referring to the sky as a loom for weaving blankets with "fringes of falling rain" and a border of the "standing rainbow."[27] The sky loom, Spinden states, refers to local desert rains that to the Indian resemble a loom hanging from the sky. Reference is also made to a "garment of brightness" with a warp of the "white light of morning." Although Tewa traditional dress is no longer worn, "the symbolical decoration on the white cotton mantle, once the regular dress but now put to ceremonial uses, is in accordance with this chant or prayer for well-being."[28] He does not, however, explain the form of the "symbolical decoration" in his note to the "Song of the Sky Loom."

VI *Quality, Not Quantity*

Alice Henderson, who lived the last nine years of her life at Tesuque with her husband and their married daughter, could have immersed herself in Tewa Pueblo culture, but apparently Native American poetic expression no longer inspired her during that period, partly due to her failing health. Although she composed few Indian poems, Alice Corbin Henderson's work presents subtle and illuminating interpretations of the spirit of Indian poetry. Since she was an experimenter, her interpretations of Indian verse were few in number, but significant in aesthetic qualities.

One critic commented, "What is poetry? To Alice Corbin Henderson it was imagination and compassion. She could be called a 'neo-primitive' in her poems about Indians and Spanish life written for *Red Earth*."[29] Several weeks before her death, nine of her friends honored her in a group of articles entitled "Alice Corbin: An Appreciation," which appeared in the Spring, 1949, issue of the *New Mexico Quarterly Review*. Witter Bynner and Oliver La Farge were the coeditors, and George Dillon, one of the contributors, was then an editor of *Poetry Magazine*. The essays were in tribute to her work as poet and editor.

Besides having compiled two anthologies of verse, one of which included Indian poems, and writing five volumes of her own poetry which showed a growth in literary power, Henderson had encouraged others, notably Lew Sarett, to create in the indigenous milieu. As an editor during the 1920s, she was also instrumental in discovering and stimulating midwestern poetry, especially from such poets as Carl Sandburg, Edgar Lee Masters, besides other well-known writers, including Robert Frost. Their work was printed in *Poetry Magazine* under her coeditorship, with Harriet Monroe as senior editor.

Despite recurrent bouts with respiratory illness, Henderson kept active in civic affairs, in literary and art associations, and in the establishment of a regional publishing house during her residence in Santa Fé. In evaluating her as an interpreter of Native poetry, her biographer, Dr. T. M. Pearce, comments that *Red Earth* "was perhaps the most original" volume of poems of New Mexico "since the author created a Southwestern poetic idiom to explore a new spectrum of imagery. As a poet she made an Anglo-Saxon reading public live awhile in the world of the Pueblo Indians."[30] Referring to the imagist movement, he concludes that the "New Poets" of the World War I era "won freedom for American poetry and were the liberators of poets of today." Among the liberators, Alice Corbin Henderson "holds a secure place."[31]

CHAPTER 7

Constance Lindsay Skinner (1879–1939)

WHILE Constance Lindsay Skinner is better known as a
Canadian-American novelist, historian, and editor, she has
written a few poetic interpretations that use Indians of the
British Columbia coast as subjects or themes. She began her literary career as a political reporter and editorial writer for the
British Columbian papers in 1895 at age sixteen, if her year of
birth is correct. Within two years she had become a drama
and a music critic, as well as a special feature writer for the
Los Angeles Times. Later she was employed by the *Los Angeles
Examiner,* and the *Chicago American.* Among her creative works,
her first play, *David,* was produced in 1910 at Carmel, California,
and *Beder of Men* was published in Germany in 1913. *Good
Morning, Rosamond* (1917), her first novel, was also produced
as a play in New York. From 1916 on, she became a contributor
to numerous magazines.

Between 1920 and 1928, she wrote four works of history and
twelve historical novels which are not within the scope of this
monograph. The histories are: *Pioneers of the Old Southwest*
(1920), a chronicle of Kentucky and Tennessee, and *Adventurers
of Oregon* (1920), a chronicle of the fur trade, appeared in the
Yale University Chronicles of America Series. Next she became a
joint author with Clark Wissler and William C. H. Wood of
Adventurers in the Wilderness (1925). Another work of non-
fiction, a history of the fur trade, was *Beaver, Kings, and Cabins*
(1933), and it was reissued in 1940. She served as editor of the
Rivers of America Series for Farrar and Rinehart in New York
in 1937, and she continued in this capacity until her death at
age sixty. As a poetic experimenter, Skinner wrote an essay on
"Aztec Poets" for *Poetry Magazine* (June, 1925) in which she
quoted from the translated poems of Muna Lee.

However, this text will be limited to Skinner's fourteen Indian
118

poems about the northwest coast dwellers which appeared in *The Path on the Rainbow* (1918, 1934 editions). Since they rank as average poems, only five excerpts are analyzed as examples of interpretations of Indian verse. She generally poetizes the Indian instead of interpreting his thoughts, his moods, or his song literature. These poems, except the three songs from the Haida, were included in her sole collection of poetry, *Songs of the Coast Dwellers* (1930).

This book contains forty-one narrative and descriptive poems reprinted from magazines. Eleven of them were from the *Rainbow* anthology: "Summer Dawn"; "Song of Search"; "Song of Whip-plaiting"; "Song of Basket-Weaving"; "Song of the Young Mother"; "The Change Song"; "Spring to the Earth Witch"; "Chief Capilano Greets His Namesake at Dawn"; "The Wild Woman's Lullaby"; "Love Song to Storm-Dancer"; and "Autumn Dawn." Her metrical compositions, she explains in the foreword of the *Coast Dwellers*, are "not translations nor adaptations of Indian poems: nor were they suggested by Indian poems," for she had not yet made a study of Indian poetry when she began to write them. But she also stated that the lyric poetry was inspired by the Squamish tribe of British Columbia. The Squamish (Squawmish) were the original inhabitants living on Howe Sound near the present city of Vancouver.

Skinner had a long acquaintance with Indian life, for, according to her statement:

I was born in an Indian country and my father knew Indians as they permit few whites to know them; and I cannot remember a time when I did not believe, with them, in the conscious earth, in the comprehending communicative friendship of trees, rocks, and waters, in the beneficence of Supreme One—nor time when I was not stirred by the rhythms of forest and river and the crashing song of the sky in the Northern Lights.[1]

I *Better Poems—Three Haida Songs*

This background furnished the subject matter for her poetry, and she evolved a theory about it. Interpretations of Indian verse are significant, she believed, because they "bespeak a native . . . American influence." In referring to the interpreter of native

poems, she says that the poet looks for beauty first, and, wherever
it is found, "he finds truth and acknowledges brotherhood." Interpreters inspired by indigenous songs have "yielded to Indian
beauty, willingly sought to enter into the Indian consciousness
and to sing of it from within, interpretatively."[2]

However, she does not strictly follow this dictum in her own
interpretations. But among her better Indian poems are three
songs from the Haida tribe of the Queen Charlotte Islands that
lie north of Vancouver Island (off the mainland of British Columbia) which are politically a part of that province. The "Love
Song,"[3] the first of these three poems, suggests the Indian's
imagery of comparison:

> Beautiful is she, this woman,
> As the mountain flower;
> But cold, cold, is she,
> Like the snowbank
> Behind which it blooms.

How successful Skinner is in entering the "Indian consciousness"
and in singing of it "from within, interpretatively," may be
judged by a comparison of her "Love Song" with a Makah song
transcribed by Densmore. The singer of "I Cannot Forget You"[4]
was accompanied by a drum in 2/4 time.

> No matter how hard I try to forget you,
> You always come back to my thoughts.
> When you hear me singing
> I am really crying for you.

It is not possible to give an exact comparison of a native love
song translation with the Haida interpretation since the source
of Skinner's poem is unknown and since it is probably purely
imaginative. It is obvious, however, that her phrasing is only
suggestive of indigenous poetic expression, for the Indian does
not use description to set the emotional tone or mood.

To understand Skinner's Indian poetry fully, one should have
some knowledge of the richness and complexity of the Haida
and Makah tribal culture. The Haida Indians, like the Makah
tribe at Neah Bay, Washington, hunted bear and sea otters,

and were fishermen who lived in rainy cedar forests close to the sea. Haida villages of high-gabled, log-plank houses were distinguished by tall, carved totem poles. Both an emblem of the owner's clan and a status symbol, the totem poles proclaimed the owner's legendary descent from the eagle, the beaver, the whale, the wolf, or the bear. Sometimes they served as memorials to the deceased. The Haida were also noted for their carved masks and rattles.

In addition to the Haida, northwest Canadian and Washington coastal tribes in general shared a similar culture of beliefs in deities associated with sky or sun. Of greater importance to them were a host of spirits who inhabited mountains, forests, beaches, and sea. Songs were frequently used in curing rites by the shamans. Other standardized rituals—the rites of passage ceremonies surrounding birth, puberty and death—were performed by priests who spoke incantations.[5] The northwest coast nations are said to have produced a high type of culture, one that ranked with that of the southwest Pueblo and the temple-mound people of the southeast. However, the north Pacific tribes practiced no agriculture nor did they make pottery. Neither were they influenced by the pre-Conquest civilizations of Mexico, but they did have contacts with the northeast Asiatics.[6]

Their indigenous poetry was similar in subject to other culture areas—love songs, mourning songs, curing charms, hunting songs, satirical songs, and many fine cradle lullabies for children. Skinner's second Haida interpretation, "The Bear's Song,"[7] is another example of a love song. It is also representative of the Indian's simplicity of expression and of his iterative type of rhythm pattern. According to the note, there is a tradition that "whoever can sing this song is admitted forever to the friendship of the bears."[8]

> I have taken the woman of beauty
> For my wife;
> I have taken her from her friends.
> I hope her kinsmen will not come
> And take her away from me.
> I will be kind to her.
> Berries, berries I will give her from the hill
> And roots from the ground.

I will do everything to please her.
For her I made this song and for her I sing it.

Although Skinner's interpretation is not based on any known translation, her poem may refer to the myth about the bear who stole an Indian woman for his wife. The note to "The Bear's Song" did not identify the "I" in the poem, but the pronoun does suggest the mythological bear as the singer.

II   *Swanton's Translation Compared*

At this point it is enlightening to compare a translation of a Haida "Bear Song"[9] by John Swanton, one of the best known translators of the northwest coast tribes, with Skinner's lyric interpretation which fails to enrich the non-Indian's knowledge of the underlying myths that inspired the songs, or the significance of the Bear cult's rites.

Membership in the Bear cult brought high prestige, and the object of all secret societies was "to bring back the youth who is supposed to stay with the supernatural being [the bear spirit?] who is the protector of his society, and then, when he has returned [to his village?] in a state of ecstasy, to exorcise the spirit which possesses him and to restore him from his holy madness. These objects are attained by songs and dances."[10] Although the general discussion on "Ceremony" is not specific about the points enclosed in brackets it is known that the totem pole makers of the Pacific were followers of the Bear cult and that bears were featured in their dances and myths. During the winter ceremonies, the Bear dancers "juggled glowing coals and threw them among the onlookers, sometimes setting fire to their cedar-bark clothes, and while the Bears of the Bear Society, wrapped in their great black bearskins, angrily clawed the earth," the people sang their bear songs.[11]

The legend told to accompany Swanton's translation of a series of bear songs relates that a man, aided by his son, built a number of deadfalls in which to entrap bears; but the animals always escaped. The hunter, becoming angry at his own inadequacy, began a fast that lasted eight days. During the ninth night, while his son lay beside him, the father died. So the son visited the deadfalls and found a black bear in the first one. After he had pulled out the dead animal, he prepared to skin it, face up. "Now when he took his knife," the legend continued, "the bear's body began to sing through him" this song, which demonstrates the native bard's use of parallel repetition as an aid to rhythm:

> Chief, chief (that I am), I am already far away.
> At the cliff, coming from my passage
>   through the mountains,
> I hold up my head grandly.
> Chief, chief (that I am), I am already far away from
>   it.
> From my blue mountain I am now far away.
>
> On the island I travel, led about proudly.
> From it I am far away.
> Chief, chief (that I am).

The "passage through the mountains" refers to a "trail from one end of the Queen Charlotte Islands to the other" that the black bears are believed to have used. Back of Tasoo harbor "there was supposed to be a hole in the mountains through which they passed."[12]

After skinning the black bear, the man's son found another one in the second deadfall, and he proceeded to skin it with the same results. The third bear skinned sang the following:

> Chief, chief (that I am),
> They say (that I have) green mountains.
> They say that I went into the creek I own
>   which stretches its length afar.
> Chief, chief (that I am).

The allusion to "green mountains" and to the creek relates to the myth of how Elder Brother danced in a marten skin "for his younger brother Black-bear, who was being killed in the deadfall, and [who] sang the same songs that came out through the hunter." In all, ten black bears were taken in the deadfalls, and "each of these sang a song through the mouth of the human being."[13]

III *Third Haida Song*

Skinner's Haida "Song for Fine Weather"[14] makes a direct appeal to the sun to replace the copious winter rains, and is phrased, to a certain extent, in characteristic sense imagery. It is an ironic contrast to the songs of the desert dwellers who invoked the rain god to bless *them* with life-sustaining moisture!

> O good Sun,
>
> Look thou down upon us:
> Shine, shine on us, O Sun,
> Gather up the clouds, wet, black, under thy arms—
> That the rains may cease to fall.
> Because thy friends are all here on the beach
> Ready for the hunt.
> Therefore look kindly on us, O Good Sun!
> Give us peace within our tribe
> And with all our enemies.
> Again, again, we call—
> Hear us, hear us, O Good Sun!

A contrast to Skinner's interpretation of the "Song for Fine Weather" is found in a transcription by Densmore from the Clayoquot tribe on the west coast of Vancouver Island, British Columbia. As we shall see, Skinner's "Song for Fine Weather" is more descriptive, atmospheric, and more artfully contrived than the Indian's typical brief, simple, stark expression.

The following literal translations by Densmore are of two very old dream songs sung as a pair to bring fair weather:

Look Down and Make It Calm[15]

Look down you, whose day it is, and make it calm.

In explaining the next song, Densmore wrote that the Indians believed the rainbow came before a pleasant day.

Send Us a Rainbow[16]

You, whose day it is, make it beautiful.
Get out your rainbow colors so it will be beautiful.

These two songs were apparently both an appeal and a complaint to the sun to drive away the persistent fogs and the heavy rainfall which plagued the northwest coastal region.

IV *Native Cradle Songs*

Lullabies were especially characteristic of the coast tribes' song-poems, and they apparently inspired Skinner's interpretations. In parts of two such poems—"Song of the Young Mother" and "The Wild Woman's Lullaby"—she has succeeded in expressing the onomatopoetic effect of Indian song. Unlike most of her work, her phrasing in these two poems is simple and free from fine writing, although the similes are rather strained by representing the wind as a bird with "song" in its "white throat" and "light" in its "sea-eyes" and also as the "sky's blue feathers":

Song of the Young Mother[17]

M'-m'-m'-m'-n! N'-n'-n'-n'-m!
Ai-i-he-i—ah-o-he-a-1-ne—
Swing my chiefling fragrantly
On the cedar branch.
Cedar, cedar, tenderly
Sway to the singing wind.
Bright flying wind, with song in thy
     white throat
And light in thy wide sea-eyes,

The sky's blue feathers on thy wing—

Oh blow, blow, gently, softly, wind,
Rock my chiefling, wind,
In his little woven cradle.

The Wild Woman's Lullaby[18]

What shall I sing to thee, babe on my back?
Song of the Eagle that mates with the storm!
Hi-i-ri-i-ki! Ri-eek!
The wild gale is weeping, driven before him
To his nest on the black lone mast of the night;
Swinging, swinging, far out, high out, over the sea!
Hi-i-ri-i-ki! Ri-eek!

V *Translation of a Cradle Song*

In comparison to Skinner's two lullabies is a Haida "Cradle
Song"[19] translated by John Swanton. The differences in phrasing
and imagery of a translation and an interpretation again become
apparent in the two types of compositions, for Swanton's translation is more obscure in meaning and lacks the emotional mood
or atmosphere developed in Skinner's poems. However, the
touch of maternal reproof that is supposed to quiet the baby
by reminding him that "he is too high born to cry in that way"
should be noted in Swanton's "Cradle Song":[20]

> Stop crying, chief's child! Stop crying,
>   chief's child!
> I do not expect that drums will sound for you, the
>   chief's child, again, for which you are moving
>   about crying.
> Stop crying, great chief's child, a child of noble
>   family sits quietly.
> Stop crying, chief's child! Stop crying,
>   chief's child!
> I do not expect that they are going to lay heavy
>   planks   for you, the chief's child, again, for
>   which you are moving about crying.
>
> Stop crying, great chief's child.

Swanton's note to this poem states that "all this refers to pot-
latching and house-building."[21] Ceremonial gift feasts or "pot-
latches" were customary among the north Pacific tribes and were
given "to celebrate any sort of an occasion." As Indian society
was divided into three classes—the chiefs or nobles, the common-
ers, and the slaves—tribal leaders vied with one another in dis-
tributing extravagant gifts in olden days, and songs of insult
were sung to each other by rival clan leaders. Since the children
of chiefs were placed high up on blankets in the center of a
trading canoe, they could watch the goings on at a potlatch or
the building of a house out of wooden planks and these sights
entertained the infant.

VI *Popular Poet of Indian Poetry*

It may be seen from the excerpts that we have quoted that the
chief influence of Indian verse in Skinner's work is one of sub-

ject and theme rather than those dominant traits of Indian verse
already discussed. This characteristic influence is found in her
entire collection, *Songs of the Coast Dwellers,* which is a popular
and anglicized imitation of Native American customs and beliefs,
even if the songs were not "suggested by Indian poems." Her
literary reputation will rest more solidly, perhaps, on her output
as a novelist, as a western historian, and as the editor of the
Rivers of America series than on her popularized interpretations
of Indian poetry.

CHAPTER 8

Lew Sarett (1888–1954)

O F all the modern poets who have written interpretations of Indian verse, Lew Sarett comes nearest, in the opinion of literary critics, to expressing the indigenous spirit. In *Many Many Moons* (1920), he endeavored to capture the peculiar influence of native thought as well as of nature in its wilderness aspects. As a result, the "poems of Indian theme in Parts I and III of this volume ... are in no sense literal translations of original utterances of aboriginal song and council-talk; they are, rather, very free broad interpretations."[1] It was not the sentimentalized, romantic type of red forest god that Lew Sarett sang about, but the partly acculturated modern reservation Indian whom he knew in the early 1900s. His knowledge of the wilderness and the American Indians grew out of his own life experience. Although born in Chicago of mixed Lithuanian, Russian, and French immigrant parentage, and reared in the slum district, he acted as a guide in the Chippewa country for nine seasons (1904-13) to earn money enough for a college course. Ultimately, the Chippewa adopted Sarett and gave him the Indian name "Lone-Caribou."

There was, however, another side to Sarett. Besides becoming a nationally lauded poet, he became a noted educator. He first studied at the University of Michigan, 1907-08. After transferring to Beloit College in Wisconsin, he received the Bachelor of Arts degree in 1911, following which he attended Harvard University from 1911 to 1912. Also in 1912, he became an instructor in English and Public Speaking at the University of Illinois. Two honors were conferred on him in 1916 at that institution—he received the Bachelor of Laws degree and he was promoted to head the Division of Public Speaking, a position he held for two years. From 1918 to 1920, he became an associate

128

professor of English at the University of Illinois; and, as associate professor of oratory, he spent a year at Northwestern University. His academic career continued there in the School of Speech from 1921 until his retirement in 1953 as Professor-Emeritus of Persuasion and Professional Speech. Another honor came to him from Baylor University, an honorary Doctor of Letters in 1926.

In addition to literary honors accorded his volumes of verse (discussed later in this chapter), Professor Sarett was called on to read an *Ode to Illinois* at the dedication of the War Memorial Stadium in 1924 at the University of Illinois. Ten years later he won the Chicago Foundation for Literature award, and he continued to contribute much verse and many articles to various periodicals. His first *alma mater*, Beloit College in Wisconsin, conferred an honorary Doctor of Humanities degree on their distinguished graduate in 1945. Between 1951 and 1954 he was a visiting professor of speech at the University of Florida, and in 1953 he lectured on northern Canada, Indians and wildlife, and literature. That same year Northwestern University honored him through establishment of the Lew Sarett Chair of Speech.

I *Achieves Literary Fame*

As an interpreter of Indian poetry, Lew Sarett was "discovered" early in 1918 by Harriet Monroe, then editor of *Poetry Magazine*. She, along with faculty members at the University of Illinois, induced the "shy, dark, over-modest professor" to show them the rhythms of the Chippewa "Squaw Dance." He obligingly sat down at a piano and played and chanted it, in Monroe's words, "like a master." Because she detected a new voice, she urged him to translate Indian songs into English free verse. The first result in this medium was "The Blue Duck," the initial poem in Sarett's volume, *Many Many Moons* (which also included the "Squaw Dance"). Happily, this poetic recognition and the publication of his book of verse occurred when both imagism and interpretations of Indian songs were becoming recognized among the literati as "The New Poetry."

Alice Corbin Henderson, herself a student of Indian rhythm in the New Mexico pueblos, says that in "The Blue Duck" Sarett " 'comes closer to the beat of Indian music than any other poet who has attempted it.' "[2] This same poem probably caused Louis Untermeyer to conclude that Sarett has been the "most successful in capturing the fluid combination of dance, time, ejaculation and occasional vivid phrase which constitute the poetry of the North American Indian."[3] Most of Sarett's Indian songs are based on the traditions, legends, and customs of the Chippewa (Ojibway), whose lifestyle as hunters of the Great Lakes woodlands has already been described. The modern Indians living in the remote forest regions of northern Wisconsin and Minnesota observed many of the old ways and inspired Sarett's chants. Densmore, it may be recalled, had translated the lyrics and rituals of the older generations.

II Many Many Moons

Sarett's first volume of poems, *Many Many Moons*, contains thirteen of Indian origin. These poems are divided into three different parts: the first and third deal with poetry based on native themes, and the second one depicts nature poetry. The reason for this division, the author explained, was "to capture something of the atmosphere of the Indian's environment, of his setting of the Northern wilderness.[4] An appendix of supplementary notes on the legends and superstitions forming the background of the Indian poems follows the third part. It would probably have been preferable to establish the atmosphere by placing the note immediately before or after the song that it supplements. If readers are to feel the spell of the wilderness, they must be prepared to understand and appreciate Indian customs. It would be better for readers to have the preparation to absorb the atmosphere of such a vivid poem as "Red-Rock, the Moose-Hunter."[5] The poem describes how the remote northern Ojibway, by imitating the moose's call, hunted this mighty monarch of lake and forest:

> Bronze in the rose-dusted twilight,
> A statue of bronze, arms uplifted,
> He stands ankle-deep in the lilies
> As rigidly fixed and as silent
> As a red granite butte on the prairie,
> As still as the dusk in the foot-hills—

Another sample is the powerfully realistic poem "The Wolf Cry:"[6]

> The arctic moon hangs overhead;
> The wide white silence lies below.
> A starveling pine stands lone and gaunt,
> Black-penciled on the snow.
>
> Weird is the moan of sobbing winds,
> A lone long call floats up from the trail;
> And the naked soul of the frozen North
> Trembles in that wail.

All of Sarett's nature poetry features his fondness for silhouette effects. In the nature poems, the mood or the thought is expressed in richly colored words. The whole is deftly wrought with the delicate weaving of a spider's web. He also achieves in most of his verse the happy union of fitting the meter and form to the sense.

III *"The Blue Duck" and Other Interpretations*

Sarett expressed in the 1920s his most original note in his interpretations of Indian poetry. The first song to bring him literary fame was "The Blue Duck,"[7] a poetic interpretation of an autumn medicine dance. A tribal custom, the note explains, was to place a crudely carved wooden duck on a pole by the shore of Half-full-of-water, a lake near the Indian village. While part of the people danced in a circle, the medicine men chanted to the monotonous beating of drums, invoking Keétch-ie Má-ni-dó, "The Big Spirit," to supply them with an abundance of ducks for the fall hunting.

Monroe crystallized the significance of the poem when she said that "it convinces one . . . of an authentic and spontaneous use of Indian symbolism, for none of its images is dragged in—all are there as an inevitable part of the life and thought of the tribal bard who utters the chant."[8] In the "Blue Duck" 's primitive barbarity; in its rhetorical repetition of images; and in its amalgamation of sound, sense, and movement, the poet has captured the emotional tone and spirit of the ceremony. This effect is especially true in such lines as the following, which should be

recited with a sustained wailing chant that steadily gathers
power:

> Then Wéen-di-gó, the Devil-Spirit,
> Whining through the lodge-poles,
> Will clutch and shake my teepee,
> Calling,
> Calling,
> Calling as he sifts into my lodge;
> And ghostly little shadow-arms
> Will float out through
> The smoke-hole in the night—
> Leaping, tossing, shadow-arms,
> Little arms of little children,
> Hungry hands of shadow-arms,
> Clutching,
> Clutching,
> Clutching at the breast that is not there. . . . [9]

Among the rest of the native theme poems in the first part of
Many Many Moons, the Chippewa "Flute Song," the "Squaw
Dance," and the "Rain Song" are realistic interpretations of the
lyric moods and rhythms of Indian chants. The "Flute Song"[10]
describes a courting custom, and the poem melodiously reflects
the cadences and pitch of the musical instrument. These opening
lines imitate the rising and falling tones:

> Hah-eeeeeeeee-oo-oo-oo-oo-oo!
> My little Pigeon-Woman,
> For you alone as I float in
> my little birch canoe in the purple twilight,
> I am singing, I am calling
> on my little cedar lute tenderly.
> For you alone, for you alone I am playing on
> my little yellow flute mellowly.

Sarett had done for the Indian in "The Squaw Dance"[11] what
Vachel Lindsay did for the Negro in "The Congo." Both poems
express racial high spirits in words that snap, crackle, and leap
in the humorous rhythms of ragtime. Both poets employ a
similar meter and rhyming couplets. The following excerpt

comes from Lindsay's "Congo,"[12] and is to be recited "rather shrill and high":

> Wild crap-shooters with a whoop and a call
> Danced the juba in their gambling-hall . . .
> With a boomlay, boomlay, boomlay, Boom. . . .

This section from Sarett's "Squaw Dance," is to be "read rapidly with a vigorous lilt and syncopated dance rhythm":

> Shuffle to the left! Shuffle to the left, . . .
> Fat squaws, lean squaws, gliding in a row,
> Grunting, wheezing, laughing as they go . . .

The dance in Sarett's poem is a rollicking social one in which both sexes participate, usually for the entertainment of the whites at Fourth-of-July celebrations. Not only is it the commonest native dance of all, but it is the one in which whites are invited to join. The white man, whom the Indian woman has chosen for her partner, is customarily expected to give some material token at the close of the dance in return for the honor shown him— usually a silver dollar or a fifty-cent piece. With much laughter and vigorous motion, the dancers stamp around in a circle to the 4/4 time of the tom-tom, and they bend their knees to the emphasis of the initial beat. In these lines, Sarett has caught the primitive rhythm of the drum beat:

> Beat, beat, beat, beat, beat upon the tom-tom,
> Beat, beat, beat, beat, beat upon the drum.
> Hóy-eeeeeee-yáh! Hóy-eeeeeee-yáh!
> Shuffle to the left! Shuffle to the left,
> Shuffle, shuffle, shuffle, to the left, to the left.
> Fat squaws, lean squaws, gliding in a row,
> Grunting, wheezing, laughing as they go;
> Bouncing up with a scuffle and a twirl,
> Flouncing petticoat and hair in a whirl.

In contrast, the "Rain Song"[13] expresses the piteous cry of the red man for the life-giving waters of the Thunder-god. This chant is based upon an ancient "superstition," according to Sarett, for the Chippewa and other members of the Algonquian-Lenape linguistic family have a belief that bits of mica—their "rain medicine"—are the scales of the Great Horned Sea Monster. If these bits are placed upon a stone beside a stream near the dancing ground, the Indians believe that the Thunder-Spirits and the Rain-Spirits, the hereditary enemies of the Great Horned Sea Monster, will lash the hated one with their storms for daring to expose himself to their gaze. In this ceremonial prayer for rain, Sarett succeeded in expressing the peculiarities of the Indian's idiom in the imagery of the Indian bard, illustrated especially well in the following lines:

> Ai-yee! Thunderer, Spirit of the Big Waters,
> With parching mouths all the children of the earth—
> The many-foot-walkers and the belly-creepers,
> The timber-beasts and the all-over-the-earth-walkers—
> All, all are calling, calling, calling to thee!
> Hear! Hear their many, many callings!
> Hah-yée! Hah-yó-ho-o-o! Hah-yó-ho-o-o-o-o!

With the exception of "The Conjurer"—a magician who works in league with the Devil-Spirits instead of the medicine man's good spirit helpers, and who through the evil spirits' aid may perform feats of magic and spiritualism—the other two poems ("Beat Against Me No Longer," an Indian love song describing puberty customs, and "Red-Rock, the Moose-Hunter") in Part I of *Many Many Moons* are more polished and sophisticated, are narrative-descriptive, and not as essentially expressive of the Indian as the one already mentioned. But each is beautifully done in its way, as the previously quoted excerpts.

IV   Ironic Humor in Council Talks

Part III of *Many, Many Moons* is devoted to a group of Chippewa monologues or "council talks," and Sarett returns to a distinctly Indian motif in these poems. This time the Indian, speaking for himself, is protesting against the white man's encroachments. Two of the poems deserve special mention for being examples of irony, but all of the poems in Part III have their merits. These two poems—"Little-Caribou 'Makes Big-

Talk,' " and "The Winds of Fifty Winters"—are chosen for discussion because of the erroneous impression among white people
that the Indian is a stolid, stoical being who never laughs or
jokes. From my own experience with the Flatheads (Salish), I
know that the Indian is very much given to laughter and pranks
among individuals of his own race. Both of these songs illustrate
this lighter side. Furthermore, both show the Indian's humor in
its most typical aspect—that of dramatic irony.

In the first poem, "Little-Caribou 'Makes Big-Talk,' "[14] Little-
Caribou, after signing the Pine Point Treaty, discovered that the
tribal allotment of land was in separate tracts and that much of
it was under water. He then asked this question:

> How can Eenzhun be good farmer!   Ugh?
> He's got-um land all over lake!
> He's got-um land all under lake!
> For Eenzhun be good farmer
> Eenzhun should be good for walking under water!
> Should be plow hees land wit' clam-drag!
> Should be gadder potato crops wit' fishnet!
> For Eenzhun be good farmer
> Eenzhun should be fish!
> Ugh!

The other poem, "The Winds of Fifty Winters,"[15] relates a
sort of "standing joke" among the Chippewa regarding a famous
old council with government emissaries from Washington. First
the Weasel-Eye, a pompous old fellow of "fifty winters," who is
inflated with self-importance because he has been chosen to be
the Great White Chief's "trusted agent," makes his big talk.
Based on the wisdom of "fifty winters," he advises the chiefs
and headmen to sign the treaty. But Thunder-Bolt, to carry his
point, uses ridicule to poke sly fun at the Weasel-Eye's "pretty
talk" by imitating his florid manner:

> The winds of fifty winters
> Have blown about my head,
> And, lo! my hair is white with snow!
> The winds of fifty winters
> Have blown about my head,

And, lo! much wisdom lodged therein!
The winds of fifty winters
Have blown about my head—
But, lo! they have not blown away my brains!
I am done!

V   The Box of God

Sarett, who believed that "no race has ever established a contact with nature more spiritual or more vital than . . . the American Indian,"[16] enlarged upon this theme in the title poem of a volume, *The Box of God* (1922), that contains twelve Indian songs. The title poem, which won the Helen Haire Levinson Prize as the best contribution to *Poetry: a Magazine of Verse* for the year 1921, shows the effect of the Indian's contact with nature upon his conception of the white man's religion by depicting a struggle in the soul of Joe Spruce, Indian, between his old pagan god of the forests and the "God who lived in a Box" (the Mission chapel). This poem, a long narrative composition, is philosophical in its content.

"Red Gods," in Part III of *The Box of God*, consists of a collection of poems based on Indian themes. They are not translations or transcriptions; they are original songs in which Sarett "sought to capture . . . something of the poetic beauty and the spiritual significance of Indian ceremonies—war dances, lullabies, council talks, and seasonal chants" as they were revealed to him during the many years he spent with the Chippewa in their native mountains and forests.[17] These poems are more artful and less primitive than the ones in his first volume of *Many Many Moons*; and, because of this artfulness, they are less effective in interpreting aboriginal verse.

"Thunderdrums,"[18] for instance, is a "broad" interpretation of a war-medicine dance performed often in the early days when the Chippewa were engaged in fighting their bitter enemies, the Sioux. Before going on the warpath, the chiefs and braves used to dance in a ring while the medicine men made the war medicine. It was believed that by their chants, in which they invoked the aid of powerful spirits, especially the Thunderbird, they could strengthen the hearts of the warriors and make them immune to death:

> Thunderbird-god, while our spirits dance,
> Tip with your lightning the warrior's lance;
> On shafts of wind, with heads of flame,
> Build for us arrows that torture and maim.

During the course of a war dance, it was customary for an individual to do a solo dance by reenacting a dramatic scene of a former battle or struggle through pantomime, posture, or gesture. The song, "Double-Bear Dances,"[19] captures the wild spirit of one of these solo dances with its staccato rhythm:

> Hí! Hí! Hí!
>   . . .
>
> Enemies near!
> Taint in the air!
> Signs on the sod!
> Ho! the Thunderbird-god
> Gives me the eye
> Of a hawk in the sky!—
> Beat, beat on the drums,
> For the Thunderbird comes.[5]
>   Ho! Ho!

In contrast to the spirited swing of the war-dance songs is the gentle note in the Chippewa lullaby quoted below. Because of the "Indian Sleep-Song" 's[20] rhythmic suggestion of an Indian mother rocking her baby in its cradle board, which is placed in a blanket hung between two poles, this poem is a fine example of a "sleep-song" interpretation:

> Zhóo. . . . zhoo, zhóo!
> My little brown chief,
> The bough of the willow
> Is rocking the leaf;
> The sleepy wind cries
> To you, close your eyes,—
> O little brown chief,
> Zhóo. . . . zhoo, zhóo!

The remainder of the poems in *The Box of God* are council talks; in conception and execution, they are also like the ones previously quoted from *Many Many Moons*. The concluding song of *The Box of God* is the "Maple-Sugar Chant," which interprets the spirit of the ceremony rather than the "specific chants and utterances, for these are few and unimportant in themselves." Since the poetic theme is based on Sarett's narrative and descriptive interpretation of the "spiritual significance of this seasonal feast,"[22] instead of being an example of the Indian's poetic expression of the ritual, the poem does not fall within the scope of this study.

VI   Slow Smoke *and Other Volumes*

Sarett's third volume, *Slow Smoke* (1925), has a particular merit of its own. The book contains many fine animal poems, and it was awarded the prize of the Poetry Society of America for the best contribution to American poetry during 1925. In the sections of the book called "Vermilion" and "Figures in Bronze," he has included thirteen songs with Indian themes. They are mainly narrative compositions, and they do not follow the Indian patterns of form or expression so closely as those in his other two volumes.

Besides his prizewinning books, Sarett had other collections of verse published. In *Wings Against the Moon* (1931), the "Water-Drums" section presents interpretations of Indian poesy. His *Collected Poems* appeared in 1941; and *Covenant with Earth*, a posthumous book brought out in 1956, is a selection from all of Sarett's poetry. (Six of the poems in it had not been published previously.) The compositions were chosen and arranged by his wife, Alma Johnson Sarett, and his friend Carl Sandburg contributed a foreword.

VII   *An Evaluation*

Lew Sarett's poetry is distinguished by its vivid imagery and by its simplicity of phrase. In his Indian songs, he anglicizes the form by including description or by creating a mood or an atmosphere; but he is truthful to such traits of Indian verse as repetition, free verse rhythm for the most part, sense imagery, and the introduction of meaningless syllables to complete the cadences of a line. He succeeded in his efforts "to keep true to the peculiarities of Indian idiom, expression, and philosophy, to the psychology of the Indian, and to his peculiar outlook upon life, and true to the genuine Indian type of today and of the past fifty years" (prior to 1922).[22] Undoubtedly, however, Sarett's original metrical verse and his dramatic flair have greater popular appeal to the white reader than the interpretative copies or the re-expressions based on ethnologists' translations.

CHAPTER 9

Eda Lou Walton (1894–1961)

ANOTHER recent poet who identified her work with Indian verse and who attained some literary significance in that field is Eda Lou Walton. She was bred in Indian terrain, having been born in New Mexico. For the Doctor of Philosophy degree in 1920, she wrote a two-volume dissertation on "Navajo Traditional Poetry: Its Content and Form" at the University of California, Berkeley. The future educator and interpretative poet had begun her work at the university at eighteen as a freshman in 1912, but had dropped out the next year to serve as head of the Music Department at the New Mexico Agricultural College in Las Cruces, 1913 to 1915. In the fall of 1915, she had reentered the University of California to resume her studies, and had received her Bachelor of Arts degree in 1917. The following year her father, a newspaper publisher in New Mexico, was elected to the United States House of Representatives where he served on the Public Lands, Irrigation, and Indian Affairs committees.

After receiving her doctoral degree in 1920, she went to Fresno State College in Fresno, California, to head the freshman English course, and remained there for three years. In September, 1924, Dr. Walton went east to become an instructor in the English Department at New York University. She continued her academic career there until her retirement. In 1928, she began serving as assistant professor of modern poetry and was promoted to associate professor of English in 1931.

Besides winning an award for her poetic talent in 1919, Walton began contributing poems until 1962 to such magazines as *Poetry, Nation, Current Opinion, Literary Digest, New Republic, The Bookman, American Mercury, Saturday Review of Literature, The Commonweal,* and *New Yorker.* In addition to her books on modern verse and her publications in anthropology and folklore

140

journals, she published "Intolerable Towers" in *The English Journal* of April, 1930; and wrote a fictional tale of the Navajo, *Turquoise Boy and White Shell Girl* (1933). *Dawn Boy,* published in 1926, with an introduction by Witter Bynner, is her only volume of Indian poetry. It includes sixty-seven Blackfoot and Navajo songs that are divided by tribe with subdivisions as to their type. Many of the poems are based on texts collected by Dr. Washington Matthews, who has been considered the greatest authority on the Navajo. He had made anthropological studies of that nation from 1873 until his death in 1905.

I   *Interpreter of Blackfoot Poetry*

Like Lew Sarett, Walton is an interpreter rather than a translator of Indian verse. Her book contains recreated songs, by which, she explains, "I mean not literal, not even free, translations of Indian texts, but rather interpretations of Indian poetic material."[1] She comments:

The Blackfoot material is largely my own poetizing of Blackfoot myths, legends, folklore, and dance songs. Much of the Navajo material is, on the contrary, very close to the original Indian texts. I have left out tiresome refrains, repetitive, and parallelistic lines. I have shortened and compressed stanzas. I have frequently dropped out all but one of the sometimes twenty or thirty repetitive stanzas, or I have combined within one stanza the meaning of several. I have interpolated lines explanatory of obscure references. And yet, despite these various alterations, I have, I am sure, been closely true to the essence, the heart and spirit of the Indian poetic conception. I have presented these poems simply and directly, without artificiality of diction, letting the beauty of the idea or symbol stand clean-cut. This method of presentation harmonizes best with the Indian texts.[2]

One reason these Blackfoot poems are interesting is that Walton is the only known writer who attempted to interpret the verse of this tribe, whose habitat is in and around Glacier Park, Montana. Of Algonquian stock, the Piegan band of the wide-ranging, numerous Blackfeet Nation had spread southward to Glacier Park from the prairies of Alberta, Canada. Another large band known as the Bloods is found today in the vicinity of Banff, Alberta; and the tribe called the "Blackfeet" (Siksika) proper wandered eastward from Alberta into western Saskatchewan from its original home on the edge of the northern forests beyond the North Saskatchewan River. Their common name may refer to black-dyed moccasins, and the Bloods may have acquired their cognomen from their sacred face paint of red earth.

Northern Blackfoot bands who lived in buffalo-skin teepees, became trappers and traded their beaver and other pelts at the Hudson's Bay and North West Fur Company posts for guns, liquor, and other trade goods. The Piegans (meaning "poor robes") were considered proud and aloof, happy and independent. They justly earned the reputation of being inveterate horse thieves and the implacable enemies not only of white Americans but of all tribesmen who were not members of their Siksika Nation or confederacy.

So important to Blackfoot economy was the horse that the Piegan had a horse-medicine cult. It is still considered the most secret and "one of the most powerful medicines of the Blackfoot," according to ethnologist John Ewers, who witnessed a Horse Dance ceremony of the horse medicine men.[3] The rites, which were formerly performed to transfer horse medicine powers, were accompanied by drumming, praying, singing appropriate songs, and dancing. In more recent years, the Horse Dance was held to cure sick people.

Songs, of course, were an integral part of all Blackfoot rituals, including the Sun Dance, their principal tribal religious ceremony. As with other Plains tribes, this annual ceremonial was held to fulfill a pledge to the sun. The sweat lodge rites, inaugurated to purify participants preparatory to the Sun Dance, began with a series of sixteen songs, only nine of which had any words. To illustrate translations in addition to Dr. Walton's interpretations, two sweat lodge songs will be quoted. While the priest held sweet grass toward the west, he sang:

Old Man (Sun) is coming in with his body;
It is sacred.[4]

Another song sung during the rites was:

Old Man is coming in, is sitting here;
He is sacred.
His robe I have taken.
He says, let us make a sweat-lodge;

> My robe I have given you;
> It is sacred.[5]

Although their folklore is rich in myths and legends, no one, to the best of my knowledge, has tried to collect or translate Black foot songs and chants, except for a few preserved by Edward S. Curtis. Only Professor Walton has essayed to transcribe several legends into interpretative verse.

II *Repetition and Parallelism in Blackfoot Poems*

In "The Marriage Dance," Walton has reproduced the Blackfoot poet's use of repetition and parallelism to secure a unified rhythmic effect. The Indian flavor is impaired, however, by the inclusion of rhyme, a device used only occasionally in Native American poetry:

> I weave my blanket red,
> I weave my blanket blue,
> I weave my blanket all my life
> Until I come to you.
>
> I bring my blanket red,
> I bring my blanket blue,
> They are the story of the wife
> The gray chief sold to you.
>
> I spread my blanket red,
> I spread my blanket blue,
> I spread my blankets for your bed;
> We belong now to you.

The Blackfoot "War Dance"[7] more closely follows the Indian motif in its repetition and in its brevity, although it also rhymes:

> The earth is my home,
>   It is powerful.
> Water speaks in foam,
>   It is powerful.
> There sits a hill,
>   It is powerful.
> I go now to kill,
>   I am powerful.

More typical of the Indian's poetic expression than any of
the other poems in the first division of *Dawn Boy*, is the "Death
Cry,"[8] because of its sense imagery, parallelism of lines, and
repetition of words. Moreover, this Blackfoot chant does not
have a consistent rhyme scheme:

> The Above, he hears me.
> The Below, he hears me.
> You hear me not.
> I cry, I call, I am alone.
> Like clouds that blot
> Sun-pictures from the pool
> My cry, my mourning tone
> Envelopes me;
> Nothing is left,
> The Above hears me no more
> The Below is deaf!

The next division of the Blackfoot songs in *Dawn Boy* contains
legends that are presented in verse, and they are light, rollicking
ditties. According to Walton:

The Blackfoot Indian has a delicious sense of humor. His myths and
legends are full of dramatic surprises in which the tables are turned
against famous hunters and leaders. His songs are often mere fun-
poking at someone's expense. The Blackfoot faces life with zest, with
a twinkle in his eye. He enjoys retelling the old anecdotes, bold
hunting tales, and the myths in which, because he is being "civilized,"
he is rapidly losing faith.[9]

Only one song, "Hawk-Face's Horse,"[10] is quoted since it is
typical of the section and is more akin to a Mother Goose rhyme
than to Indian poetry:

> Hawk-Face bought a pinto horse
> To ride as was his habit,
> He tied him up, then went away
>   Returned and found his leather stay
> Tied to an old jack-rabbit.

From the examples cited, it may be seen that the chief influence
of the Blackfoot song-poems on Walton's work is subject matter

and sense imagery rather than form or rhythm. Her Navajo verse, on the other hand, is immeasurably superior in its Indian qualities. "All the lore and poetry of this tribe," she explains, "is in the keeping of the Navajo priesthood, a very distinct group, representing the gods and sometimes identified with them. This poetry is handed down from generation to generation by word of mouth, and with accuracy, since the slightest mistake (even in a meaningless syllable) in the priestly singing of tribal song renders the rite it accompanies fruitless."[11] The Navajo have an abundant and artistic variety of poetic inspirations, ranging from their rituals to their individual experiences.

III *Comparison in Navajo Verse*

The imagery of comparison in the Navajo poem "The Lights,"[12] ranks well with modern figures of speech. Since it is also an example of a legend in verse, it presents an interesting contrast to the Blackfoot "Hawk-Face's Horse."

> The Sun is a luminous shield
> > Borne up the blue path
> > By a god;
> The Moon is the torch
> > Of an old man
> > Who stumbles over stars.

The other versified legends in this division fail to capture so completely the full essence of Indian expression. However, another fine sample of the imagery of comparison is the "Magpie Song," found in the section that contains gambling-game songs. Walton explains that these chants "are sung 'for luck' during Navajo gambling games played with a stone and a pair of moccasins. The stone is hidden by one side in one of the moccasins. The other side guesses where it is."[13] In Washington Matthews's free translation of the "Magpie Song," he comments: "The black quills of the magpie's wings are margined with white, and thus is the black sky of night bordered at daybreak; hence the simile in the song."[14] In contrast to Walton's poem, Matthews's transcription is less literally rendered:

The magpie! The magpie! Here underneath
In the white of his wings are the footsteps
    of morning.
It dawns! It dawns![15]

As we have indicated, Walton renders the same song quite literally:

In the white of his wings,
Are the footsteps of morning![16]

Oddly enough, the gambling that the song refers to was done only at night, and the words were "uttered by a player at one stage of the complicated moccasin game ... [because] ... the Navahos [sic] have a superstition" that anyone who plays when the sun is shining will be struck blind."[17] Should day begin to dawn before a lengthy game for high stakes is decided, the players darken the *hogan* and sing the "Magpie Song."

IV   *Navajo Ceremonial Songs*

Walton has included several other illustrations of the Navajo singer's power to express vigorous and colorful images of comparison. These poems also indicate her own ability to interpret the true spirit of Indian verse; they are typical of the best Indian expression in form, rhythm, and phrase:

The Sower[18]

I hold pollen of Dawn
    In my hand,
With it I sow the night;
    Over the mountain
Spring the first, pale blades
    Of the new day.

Song of an Alien God[19]

With my blade of lightning

I reap your forests,

With the breath of my wrath

I loose the flood of your white waters.

In comparison with the foregoing song, we have Matthews's free translation from the "Night Chant"—the Navajo tribe's great healing ceremony—from which Walton evidently based her "re-created" interpretation in "Song of an Alien God." Although she changed the viewpoint from that of a "slayer" to that of an alien god, she not only expressed the meaning in more lucid terms, but maintained the "spirit of the Indian poetic conception." The following Matthews translation is a two-part sequence from the "Night Chant," a long ritual poem which contains 324 different songs that the medicine men recited during a succession of days and nights. These two sequential poems are titled "A Song of Nayenez'gani,"[20] one of the Navajo gods:

> I am the slayer of the Alien Gods.
> Where'er I roam,
> Before me
> Forests white are strewn around.
> The lightning scatters;
> But 'tis I who cause it.

II

> I am the Child of the Water.
> Where'er I roam,
> Behind me
> Waters white are strewn around.
> The tempest scatters;
> But 'tis I who cause it.

Navajo shamans told Matthews that "forests white" referred to the light-colored inner surface of a tree struck and peeled by lightning. "Child of the Water" is a lesser god who is considered by some shamans to be a younger brother of Nayenez'gani, "Slayer of the Alien Gods." Nayenez'gani is likened to a giant killer, and is regarded by the Navajo as their most "potent divinity" after his mother and the Sun-God, his father.[21]

V *Rhythmic Pattern of Songs*

When Walton made an in-depth study of the form, or rhythmic pattern, of Navajo songs, she found that:

the struggle between mysticism and ritual is even more clearly dis-
cerned . . . in the form of Navajo songs [than] in the content of
[these] songs [in which] is seen the ever-present struggle between
creative mysticism and ritual. . . . The tendency to swing like a
pendulum from left to right, almost never circularly, in lines of
repetition and parallelism is very definite. The unity of Navajo songs
lies in the constant use of parallelistic lines; the variety, in the use of
different types of parallelism. The parallel lines are long and, once
the pattern has been set by the first poetic impulse, of little varied
rhythm.[22]

The Navajo bard builds a typical stanza block by block; "it
is not woven." Walton compares the final effect of the structure
of a stanza to a pattern in a Navajo blanket which has, for
instance, three black stripes first, then three rows of zigzag
lightning and cloud figures, followed by three red stripes.
Repetitive parallelism, Walton concludes, is one of the chief
traits of Navajo verse, and its form is "based primarily on
'complete' parallelism."[23] The "Chanter's Oath of Truth"[24] exemplifies these characteristics in that the unity is achieved
by the repetition of parallel lines, while variety is attained
through the length of the lines. This "Oath," a prayer, is nearly
a literal translation. The prayer is offered to the gods by a
Navajo priest who asks forgiveness before he tells the white
man any legends:

> Horizontal Woman, before you shame I have;
> Above Darkness, before you shame I have;
> Dawn, before you shame I have;
> Horizontal-Land-Yellow [the west], before you shame I
>   have;
> Horizontal-Land-Blue [the south], before you shame I
>   have;
> Darkness, before you shame I have;
> Sun Bearer, before you shame I have;
> That within me standing, with me speaking,
>   before you shame I have;
> Always you are looking at me,
> Never am I out of sight,
> Therefore truth I tell,
> Therefore truth I always tell
> My word, to my breast I hold you!

A comparison with Matthews's literal translation of this song indicates the interpretative qualities of Walton's rendition which preserves the thought content of the original:

> Earth (Woman Horizontal), for it
> I am ashamed.
> Sky (dark above), for it I am ashamed.
> Dawn, for it I am ashamed.
> Evening (Land of Horizontal Yellow),
> for it I am ashamed.
> Blue sky (Land or Place of Horizontal Blue),
> for it I am ashamed.
> Darkness, for it I am ashamed.
> Sun, for it I am ashamed.
> In me it stands, with me it talks,
> for it I am ashamed.[25]

"I, The Priest,"[26] illustrates the use of variety achieved by different types of parallelism—in this case, by contrasted sense images in the second stanza. Although Walton probably deleted much of the repetition, this chant is a somewhat rare example of the imagery of contrast that is carried through two stanzas, instead of being confined to a single line:

> I, the smiling chanter,
> Priest of the Great Night Chant,
> Come seeking you,
> Dawn-Boy,
> In the House of Horizontal White,
> I walk the trail of morning
> Seeking you.
>
> I, the smiling chanter,
> Priest of the Great Night Chant,
> Shall seek you,
> Old Man of Night,
> In the House of Horizontal Black,
> I shall walk the trail of twilight,
> In old age seeking you.

It is greatly regretted that Walton, like Sarett, did not include notes explaining the myths or traditions that inspired all the

chants. Such a typical sample of Indian poetry as the "Song of
the War-Gods,"[27] which retains all of its original quality in the
"re-creation," loses much of its value to the reader who does not
know either the legend or the significance of the symbols. In-
cidentally, the poem is a good example of the alternating rhythm-
pattern:

> I am the slayer of the Alien Gods,
> The Sun arises with me,
> Journeys with me,
> Goes down with me,
> Abides with me always,
> And never sees me.
> I am the Child of Water,
> The Moon arises with me,
> Journeys with me,
> Goes down with me,
> Abides with me always,
> And never sees me.

Matthews's notes supply the information that Nayenez'gani,
who has already been discussed, is the first and most powerful
of the war gods, and often appears in Navajo origin myths. He
is credited with destroying the alien gods or giants "who had
nearly exterminated the human inhabitants of the world."[28] This
deity also cures disease if he is properly propitiated. In addition,
either a man who finds himself confronted with danger or
warriors who are going into battle "pray and sing to him."[29]

That Walton followed the original chant closely in her "Song
of the War-Gods" may be seen in Matthews's free translation.
The idea is conveyed in his work that the god strides from summit to summit:

> The Slayer of the Alien Gods,
> That now am I.
> The Bearer of the Sun
> Arises with me,
> Journeys with me,
> Goes down with me,
> Abides with me;
> But sees me not.

> The Child of the Water,
> That now am I.
> The Bearer of the Moon
> Arises with me,
> Journeys with me,
> Goes down with me,
> Abides with me;
> But sees me not.[30]

On the other hand, the symbolism in "The Visit of a God,"[31] successfully preserved by Walton, may be guessed by the ordinary reader:

> It thunders!
> He is thinking of you,
> See he rises, coming toward you,
> Now he approaches your house,
> He enters your doorway,
> Take down from your fireplace
> His special dish and feed him,
> That your body may become strong,
> That he may enter into you.

This "song of sequence" is from the "Night Chant," the great Navajo healing ritual. It is sung outside the medicine lodge at night. "It alludes," says Matthews, "to one of the Atsa'lei [gods] without naming him." This version is freely translated by the ethnologist:

> Above it thunders.
> His thoughts are directed to you,
> He rises toward you,
> Now to your house
> Approaches for you.
> He arrives for you,
> He comes to the door,
> He enters for you.
> Behind the fireplace
> He eats his special dish.
> "Your body is strong,
> "Your body is holy now," he says.[32]

After the dancers outside the lodge have sung this song, the singers inside sing four Finishing Hymns (also songs of sequence

from the "Night Chant") of which the following is the final one.
It is quoted as a sample of the imagery of contrast which is
more infrequently used, when extended beyond one line, than is
the imagery of comparison:

> From the pond in the white valley (alkali flat),—
> The young man doubts it—
> He (the god) takes up his sacrifice,
> With that he now heals.
> With that your kindred thank you now.

II

> From the pools in the green meadow,—
> The young woman doubts it—
> He (the god) takes up his sacrifice,
> With that he now heals.
> With that your kindred thank you now.[33]

"Antithesis," Matthews explains, "is a favorite figure of the
Navaho poets, and this song contains an antithesis which we
often find in their compositions in a contrast of landscapes, of
the beginning and end of a stream in the Navaho land.... It
[the stream] rises in a green valley in the mountains where it
forms a series of little ponds ... and flows down to the lower
plains, where it spreads into a single sheet of water and sinks."
In the dry season, the stream's course leaves on the ground
"a white saline efflorescence called alkali in the West.... The
male is associated with the sterile, unattractive alkali-flat, in the
first stanza, while the female is named with pleasant mountain
meadow in the second stanza."[34] This statement accords with the
Navajo symbolism of sex.

VI *A Literary Poet and Critic*

Walton's Indian verse ranks with the better interpretative
efforts, for she remained "true to the essence, the heart and
spirit of the Indian poetic conception."[35] She has done for traditional Navajo prosody in her in-depth study of its content
and form or rhythmic pattern what Barnes achieved in her
critical analysis of American Indian verse in general. In addition,

Dawn Boy is a volume of Indian poetic interpretations of literary merit. In fact, Witter Bynner, himself a poet of national reputation, placed Walton's work in the forefront of the interpreters. She had been a member of his verse writing class in 1919 at the University of California, Berkeley campus, where she won the Emily Chamberlain Cook Prize award for the best poetry submitted by a student.

Besides her Indian poetry, Walton authored two other volumes of poems—*Jane Matthew, and Other Poems* (1931), and *So Many Daughters* (1952)—compiled the anthology of modern American poetry *The City Day* (1929), and coedited with George K. Anderson *This Generation* (1939; revised edition, 1949), which is a "selection of British and American literature from 1914 to the present, with historical and critical essays" by the editors. Since the foregoing books of verse (except *Dawn Boy*) are general collections of poems without Indian songs, they are not within the scope of this study. In addition to a distinguished career as an editor and an educator, Walton wrote more than 300 book reviews for the *Saturday Review of Literature* and other periodicals, and published scholarly articles in anthropological and educational journals.

After retiring from New York University in 1960, Walton received the John Hay Whitney appointment to teach at Bennett College in Greensboro, North Carolina. This special award was made, according to *Poetry Magazine*, to "teachers of reputation and experience to enable them to go to small colleges"[36] that otherwise could not afford to hire them. Little more than a year later, however, ill health and a broken shoulder caused her to resign from this rewarding position. Returning to her native West, she spent the last months of her life in Oakland, California, where she died at age sixty-seven.

CHAPTER 10

Conclusion

I *Stylistic Characteristics*

THIS monograph has presented a resume of the chief features of Indian poetry; it has demonstrated the preservation of these traits of indigenous poetic forms in the work of modern poets of literary significance; and it has given such explanation of the Native American's myths, folklore, customs, and metrical style as has been needed for a general understanding of native verse. After reviewing the work of the interpreter-poets and comparing it with the characteristics of style demonstrated in the more literary translators' work, we have concluded that the subject matter, the free verse form, and the rhythm peculiar to the Indians of North America have only been preserved in varying degrees in the interpretative poetry. We have learned therefore, that there are two types of poets who deal with Indian verse: those who make free translations from Indian originals, and those who employ subjects and rhythms drawn from native life and song to make interpretations of the spirit of Indian poetry.

The characteristics of Native American poetry are subjects that are close to the daily lives of a primitive people. Its stylistic traits include a free verse form, in which ideas are frequently expressed in symbol and in which the expression is always brief and often takes one of four parallel patterns; and the use of repetition and various combinations of repetition to effect rhythm. Meter in the strict sense of the term, and rhyme are both absent. Another peculiarity of Indian verse is the "recessional movement" found in the lyric types; in such poems the emphasis or emotional intensity gradually dies away toward the close of the poem. However, a "forward movement" characterizes the dramatic type

154

in which the emphasis increases toward the close, just as it does in ballads and in many ritualistic songs accompanied by dramatic gestures and actions. Another dominant trait of Indian poetry made clear in these pages is the extensive use of sense imagery.

The investigation also reveals that two tribes (Chippewa and Navajo), widely separated as to locality, have exerted greater influence than any others on the work of the translators and the interpreters. Among the northern Indians, the Chippewa have undoubtedly supplied the chief inspiration for American poets; in the south the Navajo have left the richest legacy of poetic expression. Likewise, the music of these two tribes has been the most widely exploited of any of the tribal groups.

II *Lack of Criticism*

Another finding of this monograph is that the study of Indian poetry is relatively new since much of the significant work has been done since 1910. There is a conspicuous lack of critical treatment of the subject in print. With the exception of Barnes's scholarly study of the characteristics of style of Indian verse, which was done at the University of Kansas in 1921, and an analysis of the Indian poetic impulse found in Austin's work *The American Rhythm*, a paucity of serious investigations exists.

However, in Dr. Herbert J. Spinden's "Essay on American Indian Poetry," which prefaces his *Songs of the Tewa* (1933), the noted ethnologist-translator discussed the songs of North, Meso-, and South American tribes from a historical overview; he then examined the outstanding categories of Indian poetical compositions; and he evaluated the illustrations. Professor A. Grove Day's anthology, *The Sky Clears* (published in hard cover in 1951 and reprinted in paperback in 1964), also includes some critical comment. Dr. Harry W. Paige's *Songs of the Teton Sioux* (1970) presents an analysis of songs relating to the Siouan Nation.

Of course, those treatises prepared for the Bureau of American Ethnology by Alice C. Fletcher, Frances Densmore, and by Dr. Frederick Webb Hodge, editor of the *Handbook of the American Indians North of Mexico* (first printed as *Bulletin* 30 in 1907), differ from the preceding sources as they are primarily ethnological studies. All of them contain discussions of the style and content of Indian verse, as do other more recent ethnological monographs: Ruth Bunzel, "Introduction to Zuñi Ceremonialism," in the *Forty-Seventh Annual Report* (1930) wherein she presents "Zuñi Ritual Poetry"; and Dr. Ruth Underhill's *Singing for Power: The Song Magic of the Papago Indians of Southern Arizona* (1938; reissued, 1968).

III   *Most Literary Poets*

Among the poets identified with Indian verse, the work of three literary translators is preeminent: Alice C. Fletcher, Frances Densmore, and Natalie Curtis (Burlin). Prominent ethnologists whose free transcriptions deserve honorable mention are Dr. Washington J. Matthews, Franz Boas, James Mooney, Herbert J. Spinden, Ruth Murray Underhill, and John R. Swanton. Other ethnologists whose translations have been cited in this text include Ruth L. Bunzel, Edward S. Curtis, Frank Russell, and Frank H. Cushing.

The outstanding interpreters, rated according to excellence, are Lew Sarett, whom literary critics (according to trends, tastes, and standards of the 1930s) considered to be the most successful in expressing the Indian's poetic spirit; Mary Austin, whose work is greater in quantity than Sarett's but is not so uniformly high in quality; Eda Lou Walton, a poet of genuine literary merit; Alice Corbin Henderson, another poet whose output is of high quality but who did not produce quantity; and Constance Lindsay Skinner, whose work is average although she made an honest effort to interpret the Indian spirit in verse.

IX   *Translators Versus Interpreters*

In comparing the work of the interpreters and the translators, it has been obvious that the creations of the interpreters are more polished, more cultivated in style, and more metrical in rhythm than are translations of original Indian poems. But the work of the most literary translators is also somewhat more imbued with these same qualities than are their literal translations. This observation, of course, is based on a criterion of judging the closeness of interpretations and translations to the literal rendering of Indian songs and chants. In general, though, the translations give a truer fundamental concept of Native American songs; the better interpretations, by contrast, harmonize more closely with European rules of prosody and are, therefore, more artificial though more lyrical.

If we prefer the aesthetic values in the European tradition, flavored with Indian essentials, we should read the interpretations. If we desire the undiluted essence of indigenous verse, it is approximated more exactly in the translations. It is very doubtful if any non-Indian, reared in an entirely different culture, could ever get into the native mind and express poetic ideas in the way the Indian does. Thus, interpretations can only give an impressionistic image of the original, but they do have an artistic place in our American cultural heritage.

Other conclusions of this study are that the translations of Indian poems have suggested the inherent aesthetic and idealistic values peculiar to the cultures that gave rise to them. Moreover, such translations of Native American verse have manifested both beauty and wisdom in the myths, legends, traditions, and rituals that have inspired the poetry. A meticulous study of American Indian literature may well exercise a fruitful influence in the future on the development of subsequent writing of this same type. Besides preserving the past's collective memory, the best of the indigenous poetry has prescribed high standards of tribal morality. It is hoped that American poets, including modern Indian ones, will continue to develop this virgin field; for they could enrich our poetic literature with still more of the artistic contributions from Native American songs and chants.

Notes and References

1. Louis Untermeyer, *American Poetry from the Beginning to Whitman* (New York, 1931), p. 690.

2. Mary Austin, *The American Rhythm, Studies and Re-expressions of Amerindian Songs* (Boston and New York, 1923; 1930), p. 19.

3. *Ibid.*

4. Untermeyer, *op. cit.*, p. 691.

5. Mary Austin, "Introduction," in *The Path on the Rainbow*, ed. George W. Cronyn (New York, 1918), p. xvi. Imagism was a literary movement started about 1913 in which poetic experimenters tried to depict vigorous images or word-pictures in a few terse lines of short verses. Compression was their keynote, and this quality does bear a resemblance to the primitive form of American Indian expression. Among the better known imagist poets were Ezra Pound, Amy Lowell, Hilda Doolittle (H.D.) and John Gould Fletcher.

6. A Grove Day, *The Sky Clears* (New York, 1951; Lincoln, Nebraska, 1964), p. 1.

7. Lew Sarett, *Many Many Moons* (New York, 1920), p. viii.

Chapter One

1. Alice C. Fletcher, *Indian Story and Song from North America* (Boston, 1900), pp. 114–15.

2. Unpublished manuscript from the library of the late Nipo Strongheart, Yakima tribe, Los Angeles, California.

3. Edward S. Curtis, *The North American Indians*, VIII (Norwood, Massachusetts, 1911), 57.

4. *Ibid.*

5. *Ibid.*, p. 54. The songs and music are found on pp. 54–63.

6. Lew Sarett, *Many Many Moons* (New York, 1920), p. 84.

7. Lew Sarett, *Box of God* (New York, 1922), p. 77.

8. Mary Austin, "Medicine Songs; translated from Indian originals," *Everybody's Magazine*, XXXI (September, 1914), 413.

9. Natalie Curtis, *The Indians' Book* (New York, 1968), pp. 360–61.

10. *Ibid.*, p. 362.

11. Stanley Vestal, *Sitting Bull* (Boston and New York, 1932), p. 22.

12. Fletcher, p. 126.

13. Alice C. Fletcher, "Indian Songs—Personal Studies of Indian Life," *Century Magazine*, XXV (January, 1894), 421.

14. *Ibid.*

15. Unpublished manuscript from Nipo Strongheart's library.

16. Wilhelmine Driver, *Encyclopedia Americana*, XV (New York, (1973). See "Music and Dance Section" 5 of "North American Indians," p. 24. This is a brief review of the music and musical instruments as related to aboriginal (sic) dancing. Clark Wissler, *The American Indian*, 3rd. ed. (New York, 1938), p. 154, summarized the song patterns discussed in Helen H. Roberts, *Form in Primitive Music, an Analytical and Comparative Study of the Melodic Form of Some Ancient Southern California Indian Songs* I (New York, 1933).

17. Driver, p. 22. See also Helen Addison Howard, "A Survey of the Densmore Collection of American Indian Music," *Journal of the West*, XIII, 2 (April, 1974), 84 ff., for a more expanded analysis of the music in various cultural areas.

18. Alice C. Fletcher, in Frederick W. Hodge, ed., "Handbook of the American Indians North of Mexico," *Bulletin* 30, Bureau of American Ethnology, Part 1 (Washington, D.C., 1907), 959.

19. *Ibid..* p. 960.

20. Frances Densmore, "Music of Acoma, Isleta, Cochití, and Zuñi Pueblos," *Bulletin* 165, Bureau of American Ethnology (Washington, D.C., 1957), 3–4.

21. Driver, p. 22.

22. *Ibid.*, p. 20.

23. Fletcher, in "Handbook," Part 2, 271.

24. *Ibid.*, Part 1, 959.

25. *Ibid.*, Part 1, 959–60.

26. Alice C. Henderson, *Red Earth* (Chicago, 1920), p. 57.

27. Natalie Curtis. p. 365. This poem is a translation.

28. *Ibid.*

29. Nellie Barnes, *American Indian Love Lyrics* (New York, 1925), p. 152.

30. See p. 105 of this text.

31. Nellie Barnes, *Love Lyrics*, p. 43. This poem is a translation from Frank H. Cushing, *Zuñi Folk Tales* (New York and London, 1901), p. 255.

32. *Ibid.*, p. 154.

33. Alice C. Fletcher, "The Hako: A Pawnee Ceremony," *Twenty-*

Second Annual Report, Bureau of American Ethnology, Part 2 (Washington, D.C., 1904), p. 324.

34. Barnes, *Love Lyrics,* p. 155 ff.

35. Natalie Curtis, p. 368. See also Washington Matthews, "The Mountain Chant, a Navajo Ceremony," *Fifth Annual Report,* Bureau of American Ethnology (Washington, D.C., 1887), pp. 379–467.

36. Natalie Curtis, p. 484.

37. Nellie Barnes, *American Indian Verse* (Lawrence, Kansas, 1921), p. 54. Also quoted in Barnes, *American Indian Love Lyrics* (New York, 1925), p. 30. Original in *Library of Aboriginal American Literature,* No. II, edited by Daniel G. Brinton (Philadelphia, 1883), 153. From Horatio Hale's translation of "Iroquois Book of Rites."

38. Fletcher, "The Hako," 323.

39. *Loc. cit.* Nellie Barnes, American Indian Verse, p. 26, finds in these two songs "an unusual use of incremental repetition."

40. Barnes, *Love Lyrics,* p. 168.

41. Herbert J. Spinden, "The Nez Perce Indians," *Memoirs of the American Anthropological Association,* II, 3 (Lancaster, Pennsylvania, 1908), 267.

42. *Ibid.,* p. 265.

43. *Ibid.,* p. 260.

44. *Ibid.,* p. 264. A description of the sacred vigil is also given in Helen Addison Howard, *Saga of Chief Joseph* (Caldwell, Idaho, 1965, 1975), Chapter III, "Thunder-rolling-in-the-mountains," pp. 39–42.

45. Spinden, "The Nez Perce," 263.

46. James Mooney, in Frederick W. Hodge, ed., "Handbook of the American Indians North of Mexico," *Bulletin* 30, Bureau of American Ethnology, Part 2 (Washington, D.C., 1907), 898–99.

47. Alfred L. Bush and Robert S. Fraser, eds., Introduction, *American Indian Periodicals in the Princeton University Library* (Princeton, 1970).

48. Royal B. Hassrick, "Delaware Indians," *Encyclopedia Americana* (New York, 1972). Mr. Hassrick, Commissioner of the United States Indian Arts and Crafts Board, gives a brief but authoritative account of these Indians.

49. James Mooney, in Hodge, ed., *op. cit.,* Part 1, 386.

50. A. Grove Day, *The Sky Clears* (New York, 1951; Lincoln, Nebraska, 1964), p. 126.

51. Lawrie Tatum, *Our Red Brothers* (Philadelphia, 1899; Lincoln, Nebraska, 1970).

52. Daniel Brinton, trans., "The Lenape and Their Legends,"

Library of Aboriginal American Literature, V (Philadelphia, 1883), 181–87.

53. *Ibid.*, p. 167.

54. *Ibid.*, pp. 158–60.

55. Barnes, *American Indian Verse,* p. 56.

56. Unpublished manuscript from the late Nipo Strongheart's library. This song is also a translation by L. V. McWhorter, historian of the "Non-treaty" Nez Perce Indians who engaged in the war of 1877 against United States authority, rather than be confined on the tribal reservation at Lapwai, Idaho. Northwestern Indians among the Yakima, Nez Perce, and other Columbia Basin tribes who professed a faith in the native "Earth-Mother" religion were known as "Dreamers" because their prophet, Smohalla, asserted "that divine revelations came from dreams," a common belief among all aborigines.

57. Barnes, *op. cit.,* p. 19.

58. Natalie Curtis, p. 224.

59. Barnes, *American Indian Verse,* p. 21.

60. Mary Austin, "Introduction" in *The Path on the Rainbow,* ed. George W. Cronyn (New York, 1918), p. xxiii.

61. Alice C. Fletcher, "The Hako," 300.

Chapter Two

1. Biographical data from the *Dictionary of American Biography,* III, VI (New York, 1930, 1931), 463. Besides her academic studies at Harvard, she was sent in 1886 by the commissioner of education to visit Alaska and the Aleutian Islands. The next year she was appointed special agent in July to the Winnebagos to secure allotments in severalty for this tribe, and she finished this work in April, 1889. Receiving the same appointment in 1890 to the Nez Perce Reservation, she arranged for tribal allotments and completed her assignment there in 1893.

2. *Ibid.*

3. Alvin M. Josephy Jr., et al., eds., *The American Heritage Book of Indians* (New York, 1961), pp. 247–48. The Skidi band Pawnee, Sakuruta (Coming Sun), a member of the Morning Star clan, told Natalie Curtis the creation myth. From the East, Morning Star pursued Evening Star (White Star Woman) in the West so that creation of earth people from their union might be achieved. He had first to overcome many hard things. As he approached Evening Star, earth released a flood of waters in which an open-mouthed serpent appeared ready to devour Morning Star, who sang and flung a ball of fire at the serpent, vanquishing the monster and earth's waters dried. Morning Star's song was a prophecy of the song people should sing

whenever they captured a maiden to be ceremonially slain in sacrifice to Morning Star. He overcame all hindrances, and they were a prophecy of the Hard Things that would confront man on earth. Finally he won Evening Star and their combined Power would go to earth men.

The myth symbolizes that all things needed by earth peoples are gifts from Tirawa, the supreme Creator who made the heavens and the stars, and sent gifts to earth beings through the union of Powers of the gods Morning Star, the male principle, and of Evening Star, the female principle. From their daughter Standing Rain and the Sun and the Moon's boy child sprang all people. Tirawa gave power to the stars to watch over people. For a detailed account of the creation myth see Natalie Curtis, *The Indians' Book*, pp. 99–104.

4. Alice C. Fletcher, "The Hako," 362. It was sometime during the 1890s that she recorded "The Hako" ceremony.

5. *Ibid.*, 290.
6. *Ibid.*, 27.
7. *Ibid.*, 26.
8. *Ibid.*, 287, 288.
9. *Ibid.*, 284–87.
10. *Ibid.*, 326.
11. *Ibid.*, 330.
12. *Ibid.*, 325–26. Also summarized in *The Path on the Rainbow*, ed. George W. Cronyn (New York, 1918, 1934), pp. 293–94.
13. Fletcher, "The Hako," 303.
14. *Ibid.*, 301–02.
15. Barnes, *American Indian Verse*, p. 28.
16. Fletcher, "The Hako," 272.
17. *Ibid.*, 274–75.
18. *Ibid.*, 367.
19. *Ibid.*, 365–66.
20. *Ibid.*, 283.
21. *Ibid.*, 366.
22. *Ibid.*, 18.
23. *Ibid.*, 282.
24. *Ibid.*, 283.
25. *Ibid.*, 341.
26. *Ibid.*, 343–44.

27. The historical and ethnological resumes of the tribes appearing throughout this text are based on a variety of sources, such as the various *Annual Reports* and *Bulletins* of the Bureau of American Ethnology; *The American Heritage Book of Indians*, editor-in-charge, Alvin M. Josephy Jr. (New York, 1961); Curtis, *The Indians' Book*,

Day, *The Sky Clears,* the *Encyclopedia Americana* (New York, 1964, 1972), and especially Hodge, ed., "Handbook of the American Indians North of Mexico."

28. Alice C. Fletcher and Francis La Flesche, "The Omaha Tribe," *Twenty-Seventh Annual Report,* Bureau of American Ethnology (Washington, D.C., 1911), 570.

29. *Ibid.,* 570–71.

30. *Ibid.,* 573.

31. Walter Hough, "Alice Cunningham Fletcher," *The American Anthropologist,* XXV (April-June, 1923), 255.

32. *Dictionary of American Biography,* III, p. 463.

33. *Ibid.,* 464.

34. Day, *The Sky Clears,* ix.

35. *Ibid.,* 29.

36. Hough, "Fletcher," 256. This unusual woman sent an exhibit of industries of civilized Indians to the New Orleans exhibition in 1884. In 1896 she served as vice president of the American Association for the Advancement of Science, and she was president of the American Anthropological Society of Washington in 1903. She became president of the American Folk-Lore Society in 1905. In all she contributed forty-six monographs to ethnology. A complete bibliography is given by Walter Hough in *The American Anthropologist,* XXV (April-June, 1923), 254–58.

Chapter Three

1. Day, *The Sky Clears,* p. ix.

2. Barnes, *American Indian Verse,* p. 41.

3. Frances Densmore, "Chippewa Music," *Bulletin* 45, Bureau of American Ethnology (Washington, D.C., 1910), 13.

4. *Ibid.,* 14.

5. *Ibid.*

6. *Ibid.,* 115.

7. Frances Densmore, "Chippewa Music II," *Bulletin* 53, Bureau of American Ethnology (Washington, D.C., 1913), 254.

8. *Ibid.*

9. Densmore, "Music I," 89.

10. Densmore, "Music II," 90.

11. *Ibid.,* 91.

12. *Ibid.,* 120.

13. *Ibid.*

14. *Ibid.,* 18 ff.

15. *Ibid.,* 218.

16. *Ibid.,* 42.

17. Densmore, "Music I," 150–51.

18. *Ibid.*, 151.

19. Frances Densmore, "Papago Music," *Bulletin* 90, Bureau of American Ethnology (Washington, D.C., 1929), 100.

20. *Ibid.*, 99.

21. Ruth M. Underhill, *Singing for Power; the Song Magic of the Papago Indians of Southern Arizona* (Berkeley and Los Angeles, 1938, 1968), p. 52.

22. *Ibid.*, 5.

23. *Ibid.*, 8.

24. Day, *The Sky Clears*, p. 31.

25. Various other honors and awards in recognition of Frances Densmore's unique talents included a Master of Arts degree (Honorary) in 1924, at Oberlin College, Ohio, where she had studied piano and organ at the Conservatory of Music, 1886, and a Doctor of Literature degree (Honorary), from Macalester College, St. Paul, in 1950. Four years later the Minnesota Historical Society presented her a citation award for distinguished service. She was appointed consultant at the National Archives for work with the Smithsonian-Densmore Collection, and she received an award of merit from the National Association for American Composers and Conductors. At age eighty-one, she began editing for the Library of Congress a series of albums based on her collection. The Smithsonian-Densmore Collection was transferred to the Library in 1948. Her *Songs of the Chippewa* appeared in 1950 as a long-playing record, the first of the Library's series of ten albums planned from her collection. Seven more albums were completed in the Library series in 1952.

At eighty-seven, Densmore conducted a seminar at the University of Florida in 1954. During the last three years of her life, she was busily writing many short papers about various Indian musical subjects. See also Charles Hofmann, ed., *Frances Densmore and American Indian Music* (Museum of the American Indian, Heye Foundation, 1968). This memorial volume contains a biographical essay and includes representative articles written by her, translated songs and recorded music from various tribes, and a complete bibliography of her publications, an impressive library by themselves.

Chapter Four

1. Thomas M. Pearce, *Mary Hunter Austin,* Twayne's United States Authors Series No. 92 (New York, 1965), p. 118. Some of Austin's first interpretations, like "Song of the Hills," were published in *The Path on the Rainbow* but omitted in her *American Rhythm.*

2. Mary H. Austin, *The American Rhythm, Studies and Re-expressions of Amerindian Songs* (Boston and New York, 1923; 1930; New York: 1970), p. 64, p. 173, fn. 24.

3. Pearce, *Austin*, p. 118.

4. Mary Austin, *The American Rhythm*, 1930 ed., p. 87. Same poem on p. 69 of 1923 edition. Her poetic method is further elucidated on pp. 40, 57.

5. Day, *The Sky Clears*, p. 116.

6. James Mooney, "The Ghost Dance Religion," *Fourteenth Annual Report*, Bureau of American Ethnology, Part 2 (Washington, D.C., 1896), 1054.

7. *Ibid.*

8. *Ibid.*, pp. 771–72.

9. Clement W. Meighan and Francis A. Riddell, *The Maru Cult of the Pomo Indians; A California Ghost Dance Survival* (Los Angeles, 1972), p. 6 ff.

10. Mooney, "Ghost Dance," 953.

11. James Mooney, "The Sacred Formulas of the Cherokees." *Seventh Annual Report*, Bureau of American Ethnology (Washington, D.C., 1885–86), 387–88.

12. Austin, *American Rhythm*, 1930 ed., p. 140. See p. 173, fn. 24, for her comment. These reinterpretations of the Cherokee formulas do not appear in the 1923 edition.

13. James Mooney, "The Sacred Formulas," 381–82.

14. Austin, *American Rhythm*, 1930 ed., p. 136.

15. Josephy Jr., et al., eds., *American Heritage Book of Indians*, p. 175. It is interesting to note that in 1839 Henry Rowe Schoolcraft published an essay on "The Myth of Hiawatha," which "undoubtedly inspired Longfellow's popular 'Song of Hiawatha' (1855), America's best known poem on an Indian subject," according to Day, who continues, "(It should be emphasized that the meter chosen by Longfellow was adapted from the Finnish epic 'Kalevala,' and bore no resemblance to the verse form of any American Indian tribal poetry)." Day, *The Sky Clears*, p. 27. Later Day adds that "Hayenwatha or Hiawatha [is] the great reformer and organizer of the League, who lived about the year 1500 A.D. and whose name Longfellow borrowed for his poem [which is] about an entirely different tribe, the Chippewa." *Ibid.*, p. 133. See also Helen Addison Howard, "Hiawatha, Co-Founder of an Indian United Nations," *Journal of the West* X, 3 (July, 1971), 428–38.

16. Horatio Hale, "Iroquois Book of Rites," *Library of Aboriginal American Literature*, No. II, ed. Daniel Brinton (Philadelphia, 1883), 10. After 1712, when the Tuscarora, a small Iroquoian tribe driven

from North Carolina, joined their brethren's League, it became known as the Great League of the Six Nations.

17. As quoted in Cronyn, ed., *The Path on the Rainbow,* 1918, 1934 editions, pp. 31–32.

18. Hale, "Iroquois Book," p. 153.

19. *Ibid.,* p. 37.

20. Cronyn, ed., *The Path on the Rainbow,* p. 218.

21. Austin, *The American Rhythm* (Boston and New York, 1923 edition only), p. 98.

22. Washington Matthews, "The Mountain Chant," *Fifth Annual Report,* Bureau of American Ethnology (Washington, D.C., 1887), 420. Dr. Matthews has been called one of the greatest of the early translators of Indian poetry, who combined a knowledge of Indian linguistics with a poetic talent in translating native songs among the Navajo. His success is said to have stimulated others to labor in this field. See Chapter Five on Natalie Curtis for a more detailed commentary on the Navajo tribe.

23. Austin, *American Rhythm* (1923 edition), p. 92.

24. *Ibid.,* (1930 edition), p. 118.

25. *Ibid.,* (1923 edition), p. 155, fn. 14.

26. *Ibid.,* (1930 edition), p. 173, fn. 20.

27. John Collier, *American Indian Ceremonial Dances* (New York, 1949, 1972), p. 26. Same on p. 31 of 1972 edition.

28. Hodge, ed., "Handbook of the American Indians North of Mexico," Part 2, 522. See also Helen Addison Howard, "An Introduction to Pre-Missionary Indian Religion," *Journal of the West,* XIII, 1 (January, 1974), 9–24, for a discussion of religion in the various cultural zones in the United States.

29. Austin, *American Rhythm* (1930 edition only), p. 173, fn. 18.

30. *Ibid,* (1930 edition), p. 116.

31. Harry W. Paige, *Songs of the Teton Sioux* (Los Angeles, 1970), p. 72.

32. Austin, *American Rhythm* (1930 edition only), p. 115.

33. *Ibid.,* (1930 edition), p. 120.

34. *Ibid.,* (1930 edition), p. 117.

35. *Ibid.,* (1930 edition), pp. 38, 40.

36. Day, *The Sky Clears,* p. 34.

37. Pearce, *Austin,* p. 135.

38. *Ibid.,* pp. 108–20, for a full discussion of Austin's views.

39. *Ibid.,* p. 126.

40. Dudley Gordon, *Charles Lummis: Crusader in Corduroy* (Los Angeles, 1972), p. 182.

41. *Ibid.,* p. 187.

42. As quoted in Pearce, *Austin*, p. 127. Despite the critics' pros and cons, a few belated honors came to Mary Austin when she contributed a chapter in 1921 on "Non-English Writings II Aboriginal" to *The Cambridge History of American Literature*. Mills College of Oakland, California, conferred an Honorary Doctor of Letters on her, June 11, 1928, and the University of New Mexico at Albuquerque awarded her the same honorary degree, June 5, 1933. She was instrumental in founding Santa Fé's Organization of Spanish Arts Society, 1927.

Mary Austin wrote thirty-five books, scores of stories, essays, poems, articles, reviews, even plays. A complete bibliography of her work is included in the scholarly biography, Pearce, *Austin*, along with a critical analysis of her output.

Chapter Five

1. President Theodore Roosevelt's original note is reproduced on a flyleaf following the list of Illustrations in *The Indians' Book*, as well as Curtis's dedication to the Indians, 1907 ed.

2. Biographical information about Burlin was taken from the *Dictionary of American Biography*, III (New York, 1929), 288; and the preface to Curtis, *The Indians' Book* (1923 edition). A brief obituary of her appeared in *The Outlook*, CXXIX (November 23, 1921).

3. Curtis, *The Indians' Book*, pp. 352–53. All quotations from 1907 edition. Hereafter cited as same in 1968 reprint.

4. *Ibid.*, p. 354.

5. *Ibid.*, pp. 351–52.

6. *Ibid.*, p. 102, fn. 3, paragraph 3.

7. *Ibid.*, p. 224.

8. *Ibid.*

9. *Ibid.*

10. *Ibid.*, pp. 162–65.

11. See Chapter 1.

12. Curtis, *The Indians' Book*, p. 483.

13. *Ibid.*, p. 485.

14. Harold Courlander, *The Fourth World of the Hopis* (New York, 1971), p. 116.

15. *Ibid.*, p. 216.

16. Curtis, *The Indians' Book*, p. 489.

17. *Ibid.*, p. 477, fns. 1, 2; p. 479.

18. Walter Collins O'Kane, *The Hopis; Portrait of a Desert People* (Norman, Oklahoma, 1953), p. 175. See also the detailed narration of the Snake dance legend in Harold Courlander, *The Fourth World*, pp. 82–95.

19. Curtis, *The Indians' Book*, p. 317.

20. *Ibid.*, pp. 363, 372–73.

21. Frank Russell, *op cit.*, p. 324.

22. *Ibid.*, p. 292.

23. *Ibid.*, p. 289.

24. Curtis, *The Indians' Book*, p. 431.

25. See Preface of this text.

26. Curtis, *The Indians' Book*, p. 431.

27. Ruth L. Bunzel, "Introduction to Zuñi Ceremonialism." *Forty-Seventh Annual Report*, Bureau of American Ethnology (Washington, D.C., 1930), 493.

28. Bunzel, "Zuñi Ritual Poetry," *Forty-Seventh Annual Report*, 635.

29. *Ibid.*, pp. 494, 495.

30. Bernice Johnston, *Speaking of Indians; with an Accent on the Southwest* (Tucson, 1970), p. 78.

31. *Ibid.*

32. Bunzel, "Introduction," 709.

33. Curtis, *The Indians' Book*, p. 370.

34. *Ibid.*, p. 316.

35. Frank Russell, "The Pima Indians," *26th Annual Report*, p. 272.

36. Curtis, *The Indians' Book*, p. 357. In later times this song was sung to consecrate the Navajo's dwellings also.

37. Alice Marriott and Carol K. Rachlin, *American Indian Mythology* (New York, 1968), p. 15.

38. Curtis, *The Indians' Book*, p. xxii.

39. *Ibid.*, Preface by "B. C.," p. v (1923 ed.).

Chapter Six

1. Alice Corbin Henderson, "Aboriginal Poetry," *Poetry Magazine*, IX (February, 1917), 256.

2. Alice C. Henderson, *Red Earth* (Chicago, 1920, 1921), p. 23.

3. Frances Densmore, "Chippewa Music II," *Bulletin* 53, Bureau of American Ethnology (Washington, D.C., 1913), 116.

4. *Ibid.*

5. Henderson, *op. cit.*, p. 57.

6. Densmore, *op. cit.*, p. 102.

7. Henderson, *Red Earth*, p. 23.

8. Densmore, "Chippewa Music II," p. 81.

9. Henderson, *Red Earth*, p. 23.

10. Densmore, "Chippewa Music II," p. 263.

11. Henderson, *Red Earth*, p. 24.

12. Frances Densmore, "Chippewa Music," *Bulletin* 45, Bureau of American Ethnology (Washington, D.C., 1910), 119.

13. Densmore, "Chippewa Music II," 263–64.
14. Henderson, *Red Earth*, p. 24.
15. Densmore, "Chippewa Music II," p. 114.
16. *Ibid.*, p. 113.
17. Henderson, *Red Earth*, p. 24.
18. Densmore, "Chippewa Music II," p. 216.
19. *Ibid.*
20. *Ibid.*, p. 217.
21. Henderson, *Red Earth*, p. 25.
22. *Ibid.*, p. 27.
23. *Ibid.*, p. 57.
24. Herbert Joseph Spinden, *Songs of the Tewa; with an Essay on American Indian Poetry* (New York, 1933), pp. 78–79.
25. *Ibid.*, p. 116.
26. Hodge, ed., "Handbook of the American Indians North of Mexico," Part 2, 735, 737–38.
27. Spinden, *Songs of the Tewa*, p. 94. From the poem, "Song of the Sky Loom."
28. *Ibid.*, p. 120.
29. T. M. Pearce, *Alice Corbin Henderson*, Southwest Writers Series, No. 21 (Austin, Texas, 1969), p. 39. This short biography includes a complete bibliography of Henderson's publications.
30. *Ibid.*, p. 20.
31. *Ibid.*, p. 41. Alice C. Henderson, despite her frail health, crowded a great number of activities into her life of sixty-eight years as poet, editor, and leader in civic and cultural projects.

Chapter Seven

1. As quoted in Cronyn, ed., *The Path on the Rainbow*, (1918 edition only), pp. 346–47. Skinner produced more novels than history books or poetry.
2. Cronyn, ed., *The Path on the Rainbow*, p. 346.
3. *Ibid.*, p. 158.
4. Densmore, "Nootka and Quileute Music," *Bulletin* 124, Bureau of American Ethnology (Washington, D.C., 1939; rpt. From Da Capo Press Music Reprint Series, 1972), 328.
5. I am indebted to Professor Harold E. Driver of Indiana University for his authoritative article on American Indian "Religion and Folklore," *Encyclopedia Americana*, (New York, 1972), 24–27. This concise survey is based on his volumes, *Indians of North America* (Chicago, 1961, 1969), and as editor of *The Americas on the Eve of Discovery* (Englewood Cliffs, New Jersey, 1964).

6. Josephy Jr., *et al.*, eds., *The American Heritage Book of Indians,* p. 277.

7. Cronyn, ed., *The Path on the Rainbow,* p. 158.

8. *Ibid.*

9. John R. Swanton, "Haida Texts and Myths," *Bulletin* 29, Bureau of American Ethnology (Washington, D.C., 1905), p. 94 ff., for both legend and songs.

10. Hodge, ed., "Handbook of the American Indians North of Mexico," Part 1, 229.

11. Josephy Jr., *et al.*, eds., *American Heritage Book,* p. 282.

12. Swanton, "Haida Texts," p. 98, fn. 2.

13. *Ibid.*, p. 98.

14. Cronyn, ed., *The Path on the Rainbow,* pp. 158–59.

15. Densmore, "Nootka and Quileute," p. 285.

16. *Ibid.*, pp. 285–86.

17. Constance L. Skinner, *Songs of the Coast Dwellers* (New York, 1930), p. 14; also in Cronyn, ed., *The Path on the Rainbow,* (1918 ed.), pp. 200–01.

18. Skinner, *Songs of the Coast Dwellers,* p. 13; also in Cronyn, ed., *The Path on the Rainbow,* pp. 215–16.

19. John R. Swanton, "Haida Songs," *Publications* of American Ethnological Society, III (Leyden, Holland, 1912), 28–29.

20. *Ibid.*, p. 24.

21. *Ibid.*

Chapter Eight

1. Lew Sarett, *Many Many Moons* (New York, 1920), p. viii. Of Sarett's four original books of verse *Covenant with Earth* (Gainesville, Florida, 1956), was the only book of his poems still in print in the 1960s.

2. Alice Corbin Henderson as quoted by Harriet Monroe, "Lew Sarett and Our Aboriginal Inheritance," *Poetry Magazine,* XXVII (November, 1925), 89.

3. Louis Untermeyer, ed., "Preface," *Modern American Poetry,* 4th rev. ed. (New York, 1930), p. 24.

4. Sarett, *Many Many Moons,* xi.

5. *Ibid.*, p. 22.

6. *Ibid.*, p. 37.

7. *Ibid.*, p. 5.

8. Harriet Monroe, "Sarett and Aboriginal Inheritance," p. 90.

9. Sarett, *Covenant with Earth,* pp. 82–83; also in *Many Many Moons,* p. 5.

10. Sarett, *Many Many Moons,* p. 8.

11. Sarett, *Covenant with Earth*, p. 76; also in *Many Many Moons*, p. 11.

12. Louis Untermeyer, ed., *Modern American and British Poetry* (New York, 1922, 1923), pp. 130–31.

13. Sarett, *Covenant with Earth*, p. 139; also in *Many Many Moons*, pp. 27–28.

14. Sarett, *Covenant with Earth*, p. 118; also in *Many Many Moons*, p. 61.

15. Sarett, *Covenant with Earth*, p. 113; also in *Many Many Moons*, p. 54.

16. Sarett, *Many Many Moons*, p. 84.

17. Sarett, *The Box of God* (New York, 1922), pp. 77–78. The title poem is reprinted in *Covenant with Earth*, pp. 61–75.

18. Sarett, *Covenant with Earth*, p. 86; also in *The Box of God*, p. 53.

19. Sarett, *Covenant with Earth*, pp. 86–87; also in *The Box of God*, p. 54.

20. Sarett, *The Box of God*, pp. 59–60.

21. *Ibid.*, p. 89.

22. *Ibid.*, p. 78.

Chapter Nine

1. Eda Lou Walton, *Dawn Boy* (New York, 1926), p. vii.

2. *Ibid.*, pp. viii-ix.

3. John C. Ewers, "The Horse in Blackfoot Indian Culture: with Comparative Material from Other Western Tribes," *Bulletin* 159, Bureau of American Ethnology (Washington, D.C., 1955), 257. The description of a modern horse dance is given on pp. 264 ff.

4. Edward S. Curtis, *The North American Indians*, VI (Norwood, Massachusetts, 1911), 32.

5. *Ibid.*, p. 36.

6. Walton, *Dawn Boy*, p. 4.

7. *Ibid.*, p. 7.

8. *Ibid.*, p. 15.

9. *Ibid.*, p. x.

10. *Ibid.*, p. 19.

11. *Ibid.*, p. xi. For a fuller description of the Navajo see the chapter on Natalie Curtis (Burlin).

12. *Ibid.*, p. 35.

13. *Ibid.*, p. 44.

14. Washington Matthews, "Navajo Gambling Songs," *The American Anthropologist*, II (Washington, D.C., 1889), 10.

15. *Ibid.*, p. 9.

16. Walton, *Dawn Boy*, p. 46.

17. Day, *The Sky Clears*, p. 96.

18. Walton, *Dawn Boy*, p. 60.

19. *Ibid.*, p. 65.

20. Washington Matthews, "The Night Chant," *Memoirs* of the American Museum of Natural History, VI (New York, May, 1902), 281.

21. *Ibid.*, p. 19.

22. Walton, *Dawn Boy*, p. xiii. In a letter dated at New York, March 28, 1932, Dr. Walton wrote me that "what I meant by the statement ... was that parallelism in Navajo verse is rather of the simple repetition or incremental variety a b c

a' b' c'

or

a b. c

a d c   than of the envelope or more highly developed patterns in parallelism." Parallelism is also discussed by Eda Lou Walton in "Navaho Poetry; An Interpretation," *The Texas Review*, VII (April, 1922), 208.

23. Eda Lou Walton and T. T. Waterman, "American Indian Poetry." *The American Anthropologist*, XXVII (January, 1925), 40. Further examples of "envelope," "chain," "repeating," "incremental," and other types of parallelism arc discussed in detail on pp. 38 ff.

24. Walton, *Dawn Boy*, p. 54. Also quoted with a discussion by Dr. Walton in "Navaho Poetry," pp. 200–01.

25. Washington Matthews, "Navajo Legends," *Memoirs* of The American Folk-Lore Society, V (1897), 258.

26. Walton, *Dawn Boy*, p. 57.

27. *Ibid.*, p. 66.

28. Matthews, "The Night Chant," p. 19.

29. *Ibid.*, p. 20.

30. *Ibid.*, p. 280.

31. Walton, *Dawn Boy*, p. 64.

32. Matthews, "The Night Chant," p. 153.

33. *Ibid.*

34. *Ibid.*, pp. 289–90.

35. Walton, *Dawn Boy*, p. ix.

36. *Poetry Magazine*, Contributors' Section, XCIX (February, 1962), 330. Her date of death is given as December 9, 1961, the same as reported by her literary executor, Dr. Suzanne Henig, Division of Humanities, San Diego State College, San Diego, California, in a letter to me January 27, 1970. Professor Henig comments that

Dr. Walton "apparently choked to death on some food during the middle of the night, according to the autopsy report. She was found early the next morning by her adopted son, Tom Kelly."

Selected Bibliography

Since the subject of this study is Native American verse, only the original translations of the Indians' song poems are included in the primary sources of this bibliography; all other works are considered as secondary materials. Where references contain both numerous original translations and critical or ethnological data, they are also classified as primary sources.

PRIMARY SOURCES

BARNES, NELLIE, trans. "Song of the Stars." *Golden Book*, XVII (February, 1933), 167. One thirteen-line poem of Indian origin from Barnes' *American Indian Love Lyrics*.

BOAS, FRANZ. "The Central Eskimo." *Sixth Annual Report*, Bureau of American Ethnology (Washington, D.C., 1888), 399–669.

————. "Ethnology of the Kwakiutl." *Thirty-Fifth Annual Report*, Bureau of American Ethnology (Washington, D.C., 1921), Part 1, 41–794; Part 2, 795–1481.

BRINTON, DANIEL G., ed. and trans. *Library of Aboriginal American Literature*. Philadelphia: D. G. Brinton, v. I, 1882; v. II, III, 1883; v. V, VI, 1885; v. VII, 1887; v. VIII, 1890. These volumes contain poetic translations from various tribes.

BRISBIN, J. S. "Poetry of Indians." *Harper's Magazine*, LVII (June, 1878), 104. Some translations are given.

BUNZEL, RUTH L. "Introduction to Zuñi Ceremonialism." *Forty-Seventh Annual Report*, Bureau of American Ethnology (Washington, D.C., 1930), 469–1086. This includes a study of "Zuñi Ritual Poetry," and "Zuñi Katzinas."

BURLIN, NATALIE CURTIS. See Curtis.

BUSH, ALFRED L. and ROBERT S. FRASER, eds. *American Indian Periodicals in the Princeton University Library*. Princeton: University Press, 1970. A bibliographical listing of a collection of contemporary Indian magazines. newspapers, reports, and mimeographed news sheets of 271 items from North America and Mexico. One newspaper, *Akwesasne Notes*, features a page or more of modern verse composed in English by Indians.

CASSIDY, INA SIZER. "Translations from the Navajo: 'Maid Who Became a Bear'; 'Reared within the Mountains'; 'Song of the Mountain Sheep'; 'Song of the Sun'; 'Farewell of the Prophet.' " *Poetry Magazine,* XLIII, 3 (December, 1933), 119–23. A note states that these poems, done with the assistance of a full-blooded Navajo, Henry Tracy, "may be regarded as translations."

CURTIS, EDWARD S. *The North American Indians,* VI, VIII. Norwood, Massachusetts: Privately printed, 1911. A brief account of the history, rituals, songs, and music of the Blackfoot appears in VI, all field recorded. A more extensive account of the same subjects relative to the Nez Perce, and collected from the old men, appears in VIII.

CURTIS, NATALIE. *The Indians' Book.* New York: Harper and Brothers, 1907; reissued 1923, 1935, 1950; New York: Dover Publications, Inc., 1968. Translations of narrative and poetic Indian lore with musical scores. An invaluable source book.

CUSHING, FRANK H. *Zuñi Folk Tales.* New York and London: G. P. Putnam's Sons, 1901. Contains translations of Zuñi songs.

DENSMORE, FRANCES. *Cheyenne and Arapaho Music.* Los Angeles: Southwest Museum Papers, no. 10, 1936. All of the Densmore music collection contains songs, some of which have words, some do not; some of the songs with words are translated, others are not.

—————. "Chippewa Music." *Bulletin* 45, Bureau of American Ethnology (Washington, D.C., 1910).

—————. "Chippewa Music II." *Bulletin* 53, Bureau of American Ethnology (Washington, D.C., 1913).

—————. "Choctaw Music." *Bulletin* 136, Bureau of American Ethnology, Anthropology Papers, no. 28 (Washington, D.C., 1943).

—————. "Mandan and Hidatsa Music." *Bulletin* 80, Bureau of American Ethnology (Washington, D.C., 1923).

—————. "Menominee Music." *Bulletin* 102, Bureau of American Ethnology (Washington, D.C., 1932).

—————. "Music of Acoma, Isleta, Chochití, and Zuñi Pueblos." *Bulletin* 165, Bureau of American Ethnology (Washington, D.C., 1957).

—————. "Music of the Indians of British Columbia." *Bulletin* 136, Bureau of American Ethnology, Anthropology Papers, no. 27 (Washington. D.C., 1943).

—————. *Music of Maidu Indians of California.* Los Angeles: Southwest Museum, 1958.

—————. *Music of Santo Domingo Pueblo, New Mexico.* Los Angeles: Southwest Museum Papers, no. 12, 1938.

—————. *Music of the Tule Indians of Panama.* Smithsonian Miscellaneous Collections 77, No. 11, publication 2864, Washington, D.C., 1926.

―――――. "Nootka and Quileute Music." *Bulletin* 124, Bureau of American Ethnology (Washington, D.C., 1939).

―――――. "Northern Ute Music." *Bulletin* 75, Bureau of American Ethnology (Washington, D.C., 1922).

―――――. "Papago Music." *Bulletin* 90, Bureau of American Ethnology (Washington, D.C., 1929).

―――――. "Pawnee Music." *Bulletin* 93, Bureau of American Ethnology (Washington, D.C., 1929).

―――――, trans. "Poems from Desert Indians." *Nation,* LXXII (April 14, 1926), 407. These six songs from the Papago tribe are connected with a rainmaking ceremony.

―――――. *Poems from Sioux and Chippewa Songs.* Washington, D.C.: F. Densmore, 1917.

―――――. "Search for Songs among the Chitimacha Indians of Louisiana, A." *Bulletin* 133, Bureau of American Ethnology (Washington, D.C., 1943).

―――――. "Seminole Music." *Bulletin* 161, Bureau of American Ethnology (Washington, D.C., 1956).

―――――. "Songs of Indian Soldiers during the World War." *Musical Quarterly,* XX, 4 (October, 1934), 419–25. Besides giving a documented review of the Indian soldiers' military and musical contributions during World War I, seven translated songs, composed by the Indians, are quoted.

―――――. "Study of Indian Music." *Publication* 3671, Smithsonian Report for 1941 (Washington, D.C., 1942). A handbook on the Densmore Collection prepared for the National Archives.

―――――. "Teton Sioux Music." *Bulletin* 61, Bureau of American Ethnology (Washington, D.C., 1918).

―――――. *The American Indians and Their Music.* New York: The Woman's Press, 1926; rev. ed., 1936. As the title implies, this is a general—and authoritative—account of Indian songs and music.

―――――. "Yuman and Yaqui Music." *Bulletin* 110, Bureau of American Ethnology (Washington, D.C., 1932).

FLETCHER, ALICE CUNNINGHAM. *Indian Games and Dances with Native Songs.* Boston: Birchard, 1915. Arranged from American Indian ceremonials and sports.

―――――. "Indian Songs and Music," *Journal of American Folk-Lore,* XI (1898), 85–105. Two translated songs are used to illustrate the characteristic traits of Indian songs, music, customs, and traditions.

————. "Indian Songs—Personal Studies of Indian Life," *Century Magazine*, XXV (January, 1894), 421–31. Some characteristics of Indian poetry are analyzed.

————. *Indian Story and Song from North America*. Boston: Small, Maynard and Company, 1900. Musical scores are included.

————, and Francis La Flesche. "Study of Omaha Indian Music, A." Peabody Museum, Harvard University, *Archaeological and Ethnological Papers*, I, 5 (June, 1893), 7–152.

————, assisted by James R. Murie and Edwin S. Tracy. "The Hako: A Pawnee Ceremony," *Twenty-Second Annual Report*, Bureau of American Ethnology, Part 2 (Washington, D.C., 1904), 13–372. Religion and mythology, and translations of ritualistic songs.

————, and Francis La Flesche. "The Omaha Tribe," *Twenty-Seventh Annual Report*, Bureau of American Ethnology (Washington, D.C., 1911), 15–654.

————. "The Study of Indian Music," *Proceedings* of National Academy of Science, I (1915), 231–35.

————. "The Wawan or Pipe Dances of the Omahas." *Sixteenth and Seventeenth Annual Reports*, 3, nos. 3 and 4, Peabody Museum, Harvard University (1884), 308–33. The songs are not translated.

FRASER, ROBERT S. See Alfred L. Bush.

HALE, HORATIO. "Iroquois Book of Rites." *Library of Aboriginal American Literature*. Philadelphia: D. G. Brinton, II, 1883. A lengthy ritual recited at the mourning ceremonies held for a deceased chief, it also recalls the circumstances of the Great League's founding and the names of Iroquois who were the founders.

KENNEDY, KATHARINE K., trans. "Zuñi Rituals," *Poetry Magazine*, L (August, 1937), 254–57. Based on Zuñi legends, five songs are rendered into English by the translator.

KILPATRICK, JACK FREDERICK and ANNA GRITTS KILPATRICK, trans. *Walk in Your Soul*. Dallas, Texas: Southern Methodist University Press, 1965. Love Incantations of the Oklahoma Cherokees. Translations from documents in the personal collection of the authors.

LEVITAS, GLORIA, FRANK ROBERT VINELO, and JACQUELINE J. VINELO, eds. *American Indian Prose and Poetry*. New York: G. P. Putnam's Sons, Capricorn Books, 1974. Anthology by anthropologists of myths, legends, songs from all tribal cultural zones in the United States selected from well-known ethnologist translators.

MATTHEWS, WASHINGTON. "The Mountain Chant, a Navajo Ceremony,"

Fifth Annual Report, Bureau of American Ethnology (Washington, D.C., 1887), 379–467.

————. "Navajo Gambling Songs," *The American Anthropologist,* II, 1, old series (1889), 1–20.

————. "Navaho Legends." *Memoirs* of The American Folk-Lore Society, V (1897), viii and 299 pp. Contains translation of songs from the Navajo origin legend.

————. "Navajo Myths, Prayers and Songs," with texts and translations. Edited by P. E. Goddard. University of California *Publications* in American Archaeology and Ethnology, V, 2 (1907), 63 pp.

————. "The Night Chant," *Memoirs* of American Museum of Natural History, VI (New York, May, 1902), 332 pp.

McWHORTER, L. V., trans. Unpublished Nez Perce songs from the library of the late Nipo Strongheart, Los Angeles.

MOONEY, JAMES. "The Ghost-Dance Religion," *Fourteenth Annual Report,* Bureau of American Ethnology, Part 2 (Washington, D.C., 1896), 641–1110. An authentic source of Ghost Dance songs in translation.

————. "Myths of the Cherokee," *Nineteenth Annual Report* 1897–1898, Bureau of American Ethnology, Part 1 (Washington, D.C., 1900). Although this is mainly history and mythology of the Cherokee, a few songs are translated.

————. "The Sacred Formulas of the Cherokees," *Seventh Annual Report,* Bureau of American Ethnology (Washington, D.C., 1891), 301–97.

————. "The Swimmer Manuscript: Cherokee Sacred Formulas and Medicinal Prescriptions." Edited, revised, and completed by Frans M. Olbrechts. *Bulletin* 99, Bureau of American Ethnology (Washington, D.C., 1932), xvii and 1–319 pp. Continues the wealth of translated songs from *Seventh Annual Report.*

PAIGE, HARRY W. *Songs of the Teton Sioux.* Los Angeles: Western-lore Press, 1970. Dr. Paige field recorded many Sioux songs at the Pine Ridge and Rosebud reservations in the 1960s. Developed from his Doctor of Philosophy dissertation, the monograph is largely a critical study of the modern Indian and his continuing acculturation.

RUSSELL, FRANK. "The Pima Indians," *Twenty-Sixth Annual Report,* Bureau of American Ethnology (Washington, D.C., 1908), 3–389. Also includes many translations of songs.

"Selected Poems by Students at the Institute of American Indian Arts," *Craft Horizons,* XXV, 4 (July-August, 1965). 14–15. Under the overall title, "The American Indian Student: Two Educational

Programs," fourteen poems written by students from various tribes at the Indian Arts Institute in Santa Fé are quoted.

SPINDEN, HERBERT JOSEPH, trans. *Songs of the Tewa; with an Essay on American Indian Poetry.* New York: Exposition of Indian Tribal Arts, 1933. Contains original Tewa texts as well as Dr. Spinden's translations of them.

SWANTON, JOHN R. "Haida Songs," *Publications* of American Ethnological Society, III (Leyden, Holland: 1912), v and 284 pp.

————. "Haida Texts and Myths," *Bulletin* 29, Bureau of American Ethnology (Washington, D.C., 1905), 94–99. Songs.

UNDERHILL, RUTH MURRAY. *Singing for Power; the Song Magic of the Papago Indians of Southern Arizona.* Berkeley and Los Angeles: University of California Press, 1938, 1968. A field research study of the Papago culture, myths, legends, and songs conducted by the ethnologist for Columbia University.

VESTAL, STANLEY. *Sitting Bull; Champion of the Sioux.* New York: Houghton Mifflin Company, 1932. A very readable biography of the great Sioux medicine man. Selections of his verse are credited in the Acknowledgments to Robert P. Higheagle who assisted in "collecting and transcribing twenty-five of Sitting Bull's songs" interspersed in the text of 350 pp.

SECONDARY SOURCES

Many works in this section are useful primarily for providing authoritative ethnological data, a prerequisite to an understanding of Indian verse.

ALEXANDER, HARTLEY BURR. "American Indian Myth Poems," *Scribner's Magazine*, LXXI (January, 1922), 112–14. Seven free verse interpretations based on aboriginal myths and traditions.

————. *God's Drum and Other Cycles.* New York: E. P. Dutton and Company, 1927. Interpretations of Indian poems, especially those of the Pueblos.

————. "Poetry of the American Indian," *Nation*, CIX (December 13, 1919), 757–59. Style of Indian poetry reviewed, with examples, as literature, from Cronyn's anthology and Frances Densmore's music studies.

AUSTIN, MARY HUNTER. "Non-English Writings II Aboriginal," *The Cambridge History of American Literature*, IV, 3. New York: G. P. Putnam's Sons, 1921, 610–34. Chapter XXXII contains an historical and critical article on Indian poetry, written by Austin.

————. "Medicine Songs; transcribed from Indian Originals," *Everybody's Magazine*, XXXI (September, 1914), 413–15. These are actually two interpretative poems, "The Heart's Friend," and "A Song in Time of Depression" from the Paiute and Shoshone. Both are Austin's compositions.

————. *The American Rhythm: Studies and Re-expressions of Amerindian Songs.* New York: Harcourt, Brace and Company, 1923; new and enl. ed., Boston and New York: Houghton Mifflin Company, 1930. Besides the interpretations of "Amerindian" songs, this volume contains an essay on the influence of Indian verse and a historical review of ancient European and Native American rhythms.

————. "The Path on the Rainbow," *Dial*, LXVI (May 31, 1919), 569–70. A stout defense of George Cronyn's anthology directed against Louis Untermeyer's critical attack.

BARBEAU, MARIUS. "Asiatic Survivals in Indian Songs," *Scientific Monthly*, LIV (April, 1942), 303–07. Dr. Barbeau, anthropologist and folklorist, compared customs and songs of West Coast Indians with those of Mongolians and other Orientals.

BARNES, NELLIE, ed. *American Indian Love Lyrics and Other Verse.* Foreword by Mary Austin. New York: The Macmillan Company, 1925. Poetry selected for reprint from the translated songs of North American Indians.

————. *American Indian Verse, Characteristics of Style.* Bulletin, XXII, 18, Lawrence, Kansas: University of Kansas, 1821. The most comprehensive, scholarly, critical, study extant.

BELITT, BEN. "E. L. W., a Homage," *New Mexico Quarterly*, XXXIII, 3 (Autumn, 1963), 266–71. A tribute to Eda Lou Walton and a critique of her poetry.

BOAS, FRANZ. "Stylistic Aspects of Primitive Literature," *Journal of American Folk-Lore*, XXXVIII (June-September, 1925) 329–39. Characteristics of American Indian tales and songs compared with those of all other races.

BRINTON, DANIEL G., trans. *Aboriginal American Authors.* Philadelphia: D. G. Brinton, 1883. A brief book (63 pp.) on the North, Meso-, and South American continents' native literature. No songs included.

BYNNER, WITTER and OLIVER LA FARGE, eds. "Alice Corbin: An Appreciation," *New Mexico Quarterly Review*, XIX (Spring, 1949), 34–79. A series of articles in tribute to the poet-journalist-editor by nine friends including Bynner, La Farge, George Dillon, John Gould Fletcher, Carl Sandburg, Padraic Colum, Ruth Laughlin, Haniel Long, and Spud Johnson.

BYNNER, WITTER. *Indian Earth.* New York: A. A. Knopf, 1929. A section is devoted to poetic descriptions of the Pueblo Indian dances in New Mexico and Arizona.

"Chinese Words in Indian Songs," *Literary Digest* (February 11, 1933), p. 28. Cites Dr. Barbeau's evidence in funeral chants and music showing Indians were originally a Mongolian race.

COLLIER, JOHN. *American Indian Ceremonial Dances.* New York: Crown Publishers, Inc., 1972; rpt. and rev. ed. of *Patterns and Ceremonials of the Indians of the Southwest,* New York: E. P. Dutton and Company, 1949. The former Commissioner of Indian Affairs finds a "microcosm of our whole human world in crisis" among modern southwest tribal groups, and he gives an insightful resume of ethnological data.

COURLANDER, HAROLD. *The Fourth World of the Hopis.* New York: Crown Publishers, Inc., 1971. A former United Nations editor, the anthropologist-author collected the myths and legends of the Hopi Nation during many field trips.

CRONYN, GEORGE W., ed. *The Path on the Rainbow.* Introduction by Mary H. Austin. New York: Boni and Liveright, 1918; new and enl. ed., New York: Liveright Publishing Corporation, 1934, 1962. An anthology of songs and chants (a few translations but mostly interpretations) from the North American Indians.

DAY ARTHUR GROVE. *The Sky Clears; Poetry of the American Indians.* New York: The Macmillan Company, 1951; Lincoln, Nebraska: University of Nebraska Press, 1964. A comprehensive study of translations of American Indian poetry; contains poems from about forty tribes with comments on the background and some critical interpretation of the verse. A source book of reprinted transcriptions.

DENSMORE, FRANCES. *A Study of Some Michigan Indians.* Ann Arbor: University of Michigan Press, Anthropology Papers, no. 1, 1949. This booklet of 41 pp. concerns the distribution and status of the Indians during the 1930s and 1940s. It does not include either music or songs.

EMERSON, ELLEN RUSSELL. *Indian Myths or Legends, Traditions, and Symbols of the Aborigines of America compared with those of other countries, including Hindostan, Egypt, Persia, Assyria, and China.* Boston: James R. Osgood and Company, 1884. This erudite volume also contains some translations of Indian poetry, including a few songs of the California Indians.

EWERS, JOHN C. "The Horse in Blackfoot Indian Culture: With Comparative Material from Other Western Tribes." *Bulletin* 159, Bureau of American Ethnology (Washington, D.C., 1955). Reissued 1969 in a trade edition format distributed by Random

House, Inc. A definitive study of the horse in Plains Indian culture. A few songs discussed as part of the rituals.

GLASS, PAUL, adapter. *Songs and Stories of the North American Indians.* New York: Grosset and Dunlap, 1968. Although the songs and stories are "based upon studies in the *Bulletins* and *Annual Reports* of the Bureau of American Ethnology; George Catlin, *The North American Indians,* 1841; Henry Rowe Schoolcraft, *Information Respecting the Indian Tribes of North America,* 1851–1857; and Frances Densmore, *The American Indians and Their Music,* 1926, 1936," both stories and songs are free re-expressions of the originals adapted by a music teacher for juvenile readers.

GREENHOOD, DAVID. "Eda Lou Walton's Use of Her Native Scene," *New Mexico Quarterly,* XXXIII, 3 (Autumn, 1963) 253–65. A commentary appraising the poet and her verse; includes a bibliography of Professor Walton's published writings.

HAYWOOD, CHARLES. *A Bibliography of North American Folklore and Folksong.* 2 vols. New York: Dover Publications, Inc., 2nd revised ed., c. 1961. Vol. II deals with American Indians north of Mexico, including the Eskimos.

HENDERSON, ALICE CORBIN. "Aboriginal Poetry," *Poetry Magazine,* IX (February, 1917), 251–56. In Part 1 of this essay, Editor Harriet Monroe briefly surveyed the field of Indian poetry; in Part 2, Carl Sandburg commented on four songs quoted from Frances Densmore's translations; in Part 3, Henderson announced her poetic creed for doing interpretations of Indian poems.

————. *Red Earth.* Chicago: Ralph Fletcher Seymour, 1920, 1921. Studies and interpretations of Indian poems of New Mexico.

————. *The Turquoise Trail.* New York: Houghton Mifflin Company, 1928. Anthology of New Mexico poetry, including some Indian poems by Herbert J. Spinden and Eda Lou Walton.

HODGE, FREDERICK WEBB, ed., "Handbook of the American Indians North of Mexico." 2 vols. *Bulletin* 30, Bureau of American Ethnology (Washington, D.C., 1907). Contains a brief resume of Indian poetry in Part 2, pp. 271.

HOFMANN, CHARLES, ed. *Frances Densmore and American Indian Music.* New York: Museum of the American Indian, Heye Foundation, 1968. This memorial volume includes a biography, representative articles written by her, songs and music from various tribes, and a valuable and complete bibliography of her publications.

HOUGH, WALTER. "Alice Cunningham Fletcher," *The American Anthropologist,* XXV (April-June, 1923), 254–58. Gives a

184   AMERICAN INDIAN POETRY

of Fletcher's works.

"Indians," *The Scholastic*, XXIX (October 24, 1936). American
Indian issue covering all phases of ancient and modern Indian
life.

IROQUOIS LEAGUE OF SIX NATIONS, trans. and compilers. *The Great
Law of Peace of The People of the Longhouse.* Rooseveltown,
New York: White Roots of Peace, n. d. This pamphlet, a classic
of Native American literature and art, describes The Great Law
"given to the People of The Longhouse many centuries ago,
perhaps a thousand years," which has been passed on by oral
tradition for generations of Iroquois men and women.

JOHNSTON, BERNICE. *Speaking of Indians; with an Accent on the
Southwest.* Tucson: University of Arizona Press, 1970. This book
briefly highlights many little known facts about the lives and
customs mostly of Arizona and New Mexican Indians, told in a
whimsical style. The work, however, reflects careful research and
presents authentic information. There is a brief section on
"Indian Poetry."

JOSEPHY, ALVIN M. Jr., editor-in-charge. *The American Heritage
Book of Indians.* New York: The American Heritage Publishing
Company, 1961. A good, brief reference work with some factual
errors.

KLUCKHOHN, CLYDE. "The Great Chants of the Navajo," *Theater Arts
Monthly*, XVII (August, 1933), 639–45. The author primarily
emphasized the American Indians' dramatic arts through illustrations of Navajo rituals and quoted five songs from the translations
of Washington Matthews.

MARRIOTT, ALICE and CAROL K. RACHLIN, trans. *American Indian
Mythology.* New York: Thomas Y. Crowell Company, 1968. This
volume emphasizes myths and legends rather than poetry.

MEIGHAN, CLEMENT W. and FRANCIS A. RIDDELL. *The Maru Cult
of the Pomo Indians; A California Ghost Dance Survival.* Los
Angeles: Southwest Museum, 1972. Anthropologist Meighan
and archaeologist Riddell collaborated to give primarily a descriptive and historical report of the Ghost Dance ceremonial based
on their field studies of the modern cult practices.

MOMADAY, N. SCOTT. *The Way to Rainy Mountain.* Albuquerque:
University of New Mexico Press, 1969. Writing in a poetic style,
Professor Momaday recounts Kiowa myths, legends, tribal history
as heard from the lips of his tribespeople, blended with personal
memories and experiences as a boy growing up on the reservation.

MONROE, HARRIET. "Lew Sarett and Our Aboriginal Inheritance,"

Poetry Magazine, XXVII (November, 1925), 88–95. A critique of Sarett's poem, "The Blue Duck."

NABOKOV, PETER, ed. *The Making of a Crow Warrior.* New York: Thomas Y. Crowell Company, 1967; reissued as an Apollo paperback edition, 1970. A first-person narrative of Indian psychological, religious, and social life in the nineteenth century, preserved in a field manuscript by William Wildschut for the Museum of the American Indian, Heye Foundation. John C. Ewers, Senior Anthropologist at the Smithsonian, contributed a historical Foreword.

NEIHARDT, JOHN G. *Song of the Indian Wars.* New York: The Macmillan Company, 1925. History of the Indian wars done in blank verse.

O'KANE, WALTER COLLINS. *The Hopis; Portrait of a Desert People.* Norman: University of Oklahoma Press, 1953. Ways and beliefs of the Hopi, ancient and modern, are partly based on the ethnologist's field trips.

PEARCE, THOMAS M. *Alice Corbin Henderson.* Southwest Writers Series, No. 21. Austin, Texas: Steck-Vaughn Company, 1969. This monograph gives a critically needed biographical account of Henderson, and also of her talented husband, William P. Henderson, all researched from family documents. A selected bibliography is included.

————. *Mary Hunter Austin.* Twayne's United States Authors Series (TUSAS 92). New York: Twayne Publishers, Inc., 1965. A scholarly biography of Mrs. Austin and a critical analysis of her work, together with a few poetic samples.

POWELL, PETER J. *Sweet Medicine; The Continuing Role of the Sacred Arrows, the Sun Dance, and the Sacred Buffalo Hat in Northern Cheyenne History.* 2 vols. Norman: University of Oklahoma Press, 1969. Documented, definitive record of ancient and modern rituals. Episcopalian Father Powell spent ten years in field and archival research and was permitted to witness and photograph holy ceremonies in their entirety.

"Pueblo War Songs Link Indians with Far East," *Science News Letter,* XXXIII (February 26, 1938), 133. Repeat of Densmore's report of similarities between Pueblo Indian songs and Oriental ones. No songs included.

RIDDELL, FRANCIS A. See Clement W. Meighan.

SARETT, LEW. *The Box of God.* New York: Henry Holt and Company, 1922. Interpretations from the Chippewa.

————. *Collected Poems.* New York: Henry Holt and Company, 1941. Indian and nature poems are represented herein.

——————. *Covenant with Earth.* Foreword by Carl Sandburg. Selected and arranged by Alma Johnson Sarett. Gainesville, Florida: University of Florida Press, 1956. Selections from all of Sarett's poetry, "including six poems not previously published."

——————. *Many Many Moons.* New York: Henry Holt and Company, 1920. Interpretative poems from the Chippewa.

——————. *Slow Smoke.* New York: Henry Holt and Company, 1925. More interpretations of Indian poetry.

——————. *Wings Against the Moon.* New York: Henry Holt and Company, 1931. "Water-Drums" section presents interpretations of Indian poetry, 73–96.

SKINNER, CONSTANCE LINDSAY. "Aztec Poets," *Poetry Magazine,* XXVI (June, 1925), 166–68. A prose essay written in a florid style, with quoted phrases and a note by the translator, Muna Lee.

——————. *Songs of the Coast Dwellers.* New York: Coward-McCann, 1930. Lyric poems inspired by the Squamish and other Indian tribes of British Columbia, Canada.

SPINDEN, HERBERT JOSEPH. "The Nez Perce Indians." *Memoirs* of the American Anthropological Association, II, 3 (Lancaster, Pennsylvania, 1908). A scholarly ethnology of the Nez Perce with occasional one- or two-line poems quoted.

TATUM, LAWRIE. *Our Red Brothers, and the Peace Policy of President Ulysses S. Grant.* Philadelphia, Pennsylvania: John C. Winston and Company, 1899; Lincoln: University of Nebraska Press, 1970. A Quaker Indian agent among the Kiowa and Comanche at Fort Sill, Indian Territory, who served from 1869 to 1873, narrated his experiences, observations, duties, and problems. Contains ethnological data but no poems.

UNDERHILL, RUTH MURRAY. *Red Man's Religion; Beliefs and Practices of the Indians North of Mexico.* Chicago: University of Chicago Press, 1965. A study of Indian religions compared with other worldwide faiths; this work resulted from field researches among American Indian tribes.

UNTERMEYER, LOUIS. *American Poetry from the Beginning to Whitman.* New York: Harcourt, Brace and Company, 1931, 694–705. Good digest of the history and style of Indian poetry. Some examples are given.

——————. Preface, *Modern American Poetry.* New York: Harcourt, Brace and Company, Fourth revised ed., 1930. A brief, critical discussion of Indian poetry.

——————. "The Indian as Poet." Review of George Cronyn's *The Path on the Rainbow, Dial,* LXVI (March 8, 1919), 240–41. Unfavorable critical evaluation.

WALTON, EDA LOU and T. T. WATERMAN. "American Indian Poetry," *The American Anthropologist*, XXVII (January, 1925), 25–52. Scholarly review of patterns and rhythms of Indian poetics correlated with biblical verse and with special reference to Navajo prosody.

————. *Dawn Boy*. Introduction by Witter Bynner. New York: E. P. Dutton and Company, 1926. Interpretations of Blackfeet and Navajo songs.

————. "Navaho Poetry: An Interpretation," *Texas Review*, VII (April, 1922), 198–210. "An appreciation of Navaho song presupposes an appreciation of the Navahoes; an understanding of the quiet simplicity and dignity of the life of these nature-people leads inevitably to a deeper understanding of Navaho song. People and song are one." This theme is expanded in a discussion of mysticism and ritualization and six ritualized songs are quoted.

————. "Navajo Song Patterning," *Journal of American Folk-Lore*, XLIII, 167 (January-March, 1930), 105–18. Discusses traits of Navajo prosody, particularly "parallelistic balance," and cites poetic examples from literal translations of Washington Matthews. An excellent critical study of this individual nation.

————. *Navajo Traditional Poetry: Its Content and Form*. 2 vols. Berkeley: University of California, 1920. A Doctor of Philosophy dissertation.

————. "Navajo Verse Rhythms," *Poetry Magazine*, XXIV, 1 (April, 1924), 40–44. Brief essay about metrical patterns and musical rhythms of Navajo songs compared with Hebrew verse. No poems are quoted.

"War Songs of Indians like Those of Japanese," *Science News Letter*, XXXII (July 17, 1937), 40. Report of Densmore's comparison of Indian war songs with Oriental ones brought from India to Japan. No songs quoted.

WISSLER, CLARK. *The American Indian*. New York: Oxford University Press, 3rd ed., 1938. Contains chapters on "The Fine Arts"; "Literature"; "Music"; and "Musical Instruments."

Index

Anderson, George K., 153

Austin, Mary Hunter, 24, 41, 108; creative efforts, 67-68; early life, 67-69; interpreter and theorist, 85-87; poetic theory, 69-70, 74, 75, 76; translation of "Memorial Ode," 77-78, 79, 80, 81, 84, 85, 106, 156

WORKS – POETRY:

American Rhythm, The, 69, 83, 85, 155

Baker, Ray Stannard, 68

Barnes, Nellie: characteristics of Indian lyric poetry, 30-34; summary of poetic style, 39, 40, 41, 60, 152, 155

WORKS – POETRY:

American Indian Love Lyrics, 31
American Indian Verse

Belloc, Hilaire, 68

Bierce, Ambrose, 68

Blackfeet Indians: ethnohistory, 141-42; myths, rituals, songs, 142-44; *see also* Eda Lou Walton

Boas, Franz, 156

"Book of Rites," *see* Iroquois Indians

Brinton, Daniel G., 35, 36, 37, 38, 69

Bunzel, Ruth, 100-102, 156

Burlin, Natalie Curtis, *see* Natalie Curtis

Bynner, Witter, 69, 116, 141, 153

Calverton, V. F., 87

Cherokee Indians: ethnohistory, 73-74; "Magic Formulas," 73; poetry, 74-76

Chief John Buck, 76, 77, 78

Chief Red Jacket, 76, 78

Chief Sequoyah, 72

Chippewa Indians: ethnohistory, 58-59; interpretations of songs, 130, 132-37; poetic style, 60; songs, 61-63, 85, 109-14, 155

Collier, John, 82

Conrad, Joseph, 68

Curtis, Edward S., 23, 143, 156

Curtis, Natalie, 69; early life, 88-89, 90, 92, 93, 95, 96, 97, 98, 99, 100, 103, 104; evaluation of translations, 106, 156; *see also* Navajo Indians

WORKS – POETRY:

Indians' Book, The, 88-89, 97, 106

Cushing, Frank H., 156

Day, A. Grove, 56-57, 85, 89, 155

Delaware Indians: ethnohistory, 35-37; epic poem, 37-39

Densmore, Frances, 27; early life, 58-59, 60; healing songs, 64; love songs, 63-64; summary of her contributions, 66, 69, 83, 165n25; translations of Chippewa songs, 109-13, 120, 124-25, 130, 155, 156

WORKS – POETRY:

"Chippewa Music," *Bulletin* 45, Bureau of American Ethnology

"Chippewa Music II," *Bulletin* 53, Bureau of American Ethnology

"Nootka and Quileute Music," *Bulletin* 124, Bureau of American Ethnology

"Papago Music," *Bulletin* 90, Bureau of American Ethnology

188